THE AMERICAN NEGRO

HIS HISTORY AND LITERATURE

THE FACTS
OF RECONSTRUCTION

John R. Lynch

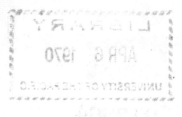

ARNO PRESS and THE NEW YORK TIMES
NEW YORK 1968

General Editor
WILLIAM LOREN KATZ

JOHN R. LYNCH WAS ONE OF THE MOST TALENTED Negro political leaders of his time. Born a slave in 1847 (his father was a white man), he became free in 1863 when Union forces occupied Natchez, Mississippi. Lynch had a few months' formal schooling, but like Abraham Lincoln, was largely self-taught. He learned photography, a difficult art in those days, and became manager of a prosperous photographic studio in Natchez. He went into politics after passage of the Reconstruction Acts of 1867, and was appointed Justice of the Peace by the first Republican Governor of Mississippi. In 1869 he was elected to the state House of Representatives, and in 1871, at the age of 24, he became Speaker of the House. He won election to Congress in 1872 (one of twenty-two Negroes to serve in Congress between 1870 and 1901), and during his two full terms in Washington had more influence at the White House than any other black man until modern times. In Congress, Lynch spoke out for the passage of the 1875 Civil Rights Act banning discrimination in public accommodations (declared unconstitutional in 1883), and urged the enactment of stronger enforcement legislation to protect equal rights in the South.

The violent overthrow of Republican government in Mississippi in 1875 ended his Congressional career (except for one additional year, 1882–83, the result of his winning a disputed election), but he remained active in politics for the rest of his life. He was a delegate from Mississippi to five Republican National Conventions, serving as temporary chairman of the 1884 convention, an honor accorded no other Negro before or since. Lynch held appointive offices in the federal government and the army under Presidents Harrison, McKinley, Roosevelt, and Taft. In 1911 he moved to Chicago, where he practiced law for twenty-five years. He died in 1939.

The Facts of Reconstruction, first published in 1913, was a reasoned and informed defense of Reconstruction against a rising tide of historical criticism. Following the lead of such men as James Ford Rhodes and William A. Dunning, historians between 1900 and 1930 created an image of Reconstruction that was dominated by greedy carpetbaggers, rascally scalawags, and ignorant, degraded Negroes. Lynch's book, semi-autobiographical in nature and concerned largely with Mississippi, provided a much-needed corrective to these unfair interpretations. *The Facts of Reconstruction,* which attracted limited attention when it first appeared, stands up well in the light of modern scholarship and must be regarded as an important landmark in the historiography of Reconstruction.

James M. McPherson
DEPARTMENT OF HISTORY
PRINCETON UNIVERSITY

THE FACTS
OF RECONSTRUCTION

John R. Lynch

THE FACTS
OF RECONSTRUCTION

BY

JOHN R. LYNCH

Formerly Member of Congress from Mississippi; Formerly
Temporary Chairman of the Republican National
Convention of 1884; Formerly Fourth
Auditor of the United States
Treasury

NEW YORK
THE NEALE PUBLISHING COMPANY
1913

CONTENTS

CONTENTS

PREFACE

The author of this book is one of the few remaining links in the chain by which the present generation is connected with the reconstruction period, — the most important and eventful period in our country's history.

What is herein recorded is based upon the author's own knowledge, contact and experience. Very much, of course, has been written and published about reconstruction, but most of it is superficial and unreliable; and, besides, nearly all of it has been written in such a style and tone as to make the alleged facts related harmonize with what was believed to be demanded by public sentiment. The author of this work has endeavored to present *facts* as they were and are, rather than as he would like to have them, and to set them down without the slightest regard to their effect upon the public mind, except so far as that mind may be influenced by the truth, the whole truth and nothing but the truth. In his efforts along these lines he has endeavored to give expression to his ideas, opinions and convictions in language that is moderate and devoid of bitterness, and entirely free from race prejudice, sectional animosity, or partisan bias. Whether or not he has succeeded in doing

so he is willing to leave to the considerate judgment
and impartial decision of those who may take the
time to read what is here recorded.   In writing what
is to be found in these pages, the author has made
no effort to draw upon the imagination, nor to gratify
the wishes of those whose chief ambition is to magnify the faults and deficiencies in some and to extol
the good and commendable traits and qualities in
others.   In other words, his chief purpose has been
to furnish the readers and students of the present
generation with a true, candid and impartial statement of material and important facts based upon his
own personal knowledge and experience, with such
comments as in his judgment the occasion and circumstances warranted.

Was the enfranchisement of the black men at the
South by act of Congress a grave mistake?

Were the reconstructed State Governments that
were organized as a result thereof a disappointment
and a failure?

Was the Fifteenth Amendment to the Federal
Constitution premature and unwise?

An affirmative answer to the above questions will
be found in nearly everything that has been written
about Reconstruction during the last quarter of a
century.   The main purpose of 'this work is to present
the other side; but, in doing so, the author indulges
the hope that those who may read these chapters will
find that no extravagant and exaggerated statements

have been made, and that there has been no effort
to conceal, excuse, or justify any act that was questionable or wrong. It will be seen that the primary
object the author has sought to accomplish, is to
bring to public notice those things that were commendable and meritorious, to prevent the publication
of which seems to have been the primary purpose of
nearly all who have thus far written upon that important subject.

But again, the question may be asked, if the reconstructed State Governments that were organized
and brought into existence under the Congressional
Plan of Reconstruction were not a disappointment
and a failure, why is it that they could not and did
not stand the test of time? The author hopes and
believes that the reader will find in one of the chapters of this book a complete and satisfactory answer
to that question.

It will be seen that the State of Mississippi is made
the pivotal one in the presentation of the facts and
historical points touched upon in this work; but that
is because Mississippi was the field of the author's political activities. That State, however, was largely
typical, hence what was true of that one was, in the
main, true of all the other reconstructed States.

The author was a member of Congress during the
settlement of the controversy between Hayes' and
Tilden for the Presidency of the United States, resulting from the close and doubtful election of 1876,

— a controversy that was finally decided through the medium of the Electoral Commission. The reader will find in the chapter on that subject many important facts and incidents not heretofore published.

Why was it that the able and brilliant statesman from Maine, James G. Blaine, died, as did Henry Clay, without having reached the acme of his ambition,— the Presidency of the United States? Why was he defeated for the Republican Presidential nomination in 1876,— the only time when it was possible for him to be elected, and defeated for the election in 1884,— the only time when it was possible for him to be nominated? The answer to these questions will be found in this book.

Then the interviews between the author and Presidents Grant and Cleveland, and Secretaries Blaine, Lamar, and Gresham will no doubt be interesting, if not instructive.

If, in writing this book, the author shall have succeeded in placing before the public accurate and trustworthy information relative to Reconstruction, his highest ambition will have been fully gratified, his sense of justice entirely satisfied.

JOHN R. LYNCH.

THE FACTS
OF RECONSTRUCTION

CHAPTER I

The year 1866 was an eventful one in the history
of this country. A bitter war was in progress between Congress and President Andrew Johnson
over the question of the reconstruction of the States
lately in rebellion against the National Government.
The President had inaugurated a policy of his own
that proved to be very unpopular at the North.
He had pardoned nearly all the leaders in the rebellion through the medium of amnesty proclama-
tions. In each rebel State he had appointed a pro-
visional governor under whose direction Legislatures, State officers, and members of Congress had
been chosen, and the Legislatures thus chosen
elected the United States Senators for the Southern
States in accordance with the President's plan of
reconstruction. To make restoration to the Union

full and complete nothing remained to be done but to admit to their seats the Senators and Representatives that had been chosen. In the mean time these different Legislatures had enacted laws which virtually re-enslaved those that had been emancipated in their respective States. For this the North would not stand. Sentiment in that section demanded not only justice and fair treatment for the newly emancipated race but also an emancipation that should be thorough and complete, not merely theoretical and nominal.

The fact was recognized and appreciated that the colored people had been loyal to the Union and faithful to the flag of their country and that they had rendered valuable assistance in putting down the rebellion. From a standpoint of gratitude, if not of justice, the sentiment of the North at that time was in favor of fair play for the colored people of the South. But the President would not yield to what was generally believed to be the dominant sentiment of the North on the question of reconstruction. He insisted that the leaders of the Republican party in Congress did not represent the true sentiment of the country, so he boldly determined to antagonize the leaders in Congress, and to present their differences to the court of public opinion at the approaching Congressional elections. The issue was thus joined and the people were called upon to render judgment in the election of members of Congress in the fall of 1866. The President, with the solid support of the Democrats and a small minority of the Republicans, made a brave and gallant fight. The result, however, was a crushing defeat for him and a national repudiation of his plan of reconstruction.

Notwithstanding this defeat the President refused to yield, continuing the fight with Congress which finally resulted in his impeachment by the House of Representatives for high Crimes and Misdemeanors in office and in his trial by the Senate sitting as a High Court for that purpose. When the vote of the court was taken the President was saved from conviction and from removal from office by the narrow margin of one vote,— a sufficient number of Republican Senators having voted with the Democrats to prevent conviction. It was believed by many at the time that some of the Republican Senators that voted for acquittal did so chiefly on account of their antipathy to the man who would succeed to the Presidency in the event of the conviction of the President.. This man was Senator Benjamin Wade, of Ohio,— President *pro tem.* of the Senate,— who, as the law then stood, would have succeeded to the Presidency in the event of a vacancy in that office from any cause.`

Senator Wade was an able man, but there were others who were much more brilliant. He was a strong party man. He had no patience with those who claimed to be Republicans and yet refused to abide by the decision of the majority of the party organization unless that decision should be what they wanted. In short, he was an organization Republican,— what has since been characterized by some as a machine man,— the sort of active and aggressive man that would be likely to make for himself enemies of men in his own organization who were afraid of his great power and influence, and jealous of him as a political rival. That some of his senatorial Republican associates should feel that the best service they could render their country would be to do all in their power to prevent such a man from being elevated to the Presidency was, perhaps, perfectly natural: for while they knew that he was a strong and able man, they also knew that, according to his convictions of party duty and party obligations, he firmly believed that he who served his party best served his country best. In giving expression to his views and convictions, as he usually did with force and vigor, he was not always considerate of the wishes and feelings of those with whom he did not agree. That he would have given the country an able administration is the concurrent opinion of those who knew him best.

While President Johnson was retained in office he was practically shorn of the greater part of the power and patronage that attaches to the office. This was done through the passage of a bill, over

the president's veto, known as the Tenure of Office
Act. The constitutionality of this act, which
greatly curtailed the power of the President to make
removals from office, was seriously questioned at
the time, but it was passed as a political necessity,
— to meet an unusual and unexpected emergency
that seemed to threaten the peace and tranquillity
of the country and practically to nullify the fruits
of the victory which had been won on the field of
battle. The law was repealed or materially modified as soon as President Johnson retired from
office. The President also vetoed all the reconstruction bills,— bills conferring suffrage on the
colored men in the States that were to be reconstructed,—that passed Congress; but they were
promptly passed over the veto.

The rejection by the country of the Johnson plan
of reconstruction, had clearly demonstrated that no
halfway measures were possible. If the colored
men were not enfranchised then the Johnson plan
might as well be accepted. The Republican or
Union white men at the South were not sufficient
in numbers to make their power or influence felt.
The necessities of the situation, therefore, left no
alternative but the enfranchisement of the blacks.
It was ascertained and acknowledged that to make
possible the reconstruction of the States lately in
rebellion, in accordance with the plan which had
met with the emphatic approval of the North, the

enfranchisement of the blacks in the States to be reconstructed was an absolute necessity.

The first election held in Mississippi under the Reconstruction Acts took place in 1867, when delegates to a Constitutional Convention were elected to frame a new Constitution. The Democrats decided to adopt what they declared to be a policy of " Masterly Inactivity," that is, to refrain from taking any part in the election and to allow it to go by default. The result was that the Republicans had a large majority of the delegates, only a few counties having elected Democratic delegates. The only reason that there were any Democrats in the Convention at all was that the party was not unanimous in the adoption of the policy of " Masterly Inactivity," and consequently did not adhere to it. The Democrats in a few counties in the State rejected the advice and repudiated the action of the State Convention of their party on this point. The result was that a few very able men were elected to the convention as Democrats,— such men, for instance, as John W. C. Watson, and William M. Compton, of Marshall County, and William L. Hemingway, of Carroll, who was elected State Treasurer by the Democrats in 1875, and to whom a more extended reference will be made in a subsequent chapter.

The result of the election made it clear that if the Democratic organization in the State had adopted the course that was pursued by the members of that party in the counties by which the action of their State Convention was repudiated, the Democrats would have had at least a large and influential minority of the delegates, which would have resulted in the framing of a constitution that would have been much more acceptable to the members of that party than the one that was finally agreed upon by the majority of the members of that body. But the Democratic party in the State was governed and controlled by the radical element of that organization,— an element which took the position that no respectable white Democrat could afford to participate in an election in which colored men were allowed to vote.   To do so, they held, would not only be humiliating to the pride of the white men, but the contamination would be unwise if not dangerous.   Besides, they were firm in the belief and honest in the conviction that the country would ultimately repudiate the Congressional Plan of Reconstruction, and that in the mean time it would be both safe and wise for them to give expression to their objections to it and abhorrence of it by pursuing a course of masterly inactivity.   The liberal and conservative element in the party was so bitterly opposed to this course that in spite of the action of the State Convention several counties, as has been already stated, bolted the action of the convention and took part in the election.

Of the Republican membership of the Constitutional Convention a large majority were white men, — many of them natives of the State and a number of others, though born elsewhere, residents in the State for many years preceding the war of the Rebellion. My own county, Adams (Natchez), in which the colored voters were largely in the majority, and which was entitled to three delegates in the convention, elected two white men,— E. J. Castello, and Fred Parsons,— and one colored man, H. P. Jacobs, a Baptist preacher. Throughout the State the proportion was about the same. This was a great disappointment to the dominating element in the Democratic party, who had hoped and expected, through their policy of " Masterly Inactivity " and intimidation of white men, that the convention would be composed almost exclusively of illiterate and inexperienced colored men. Although a minor at that time, I took an active part in the local politics of my county, and, being a member of a Republican club that had been organized at Natchez, I was frequently called upon to address the members at its weekly meetings.

When the State Constitution was submitted to a popular vote for ratification or rejection I took an active part in the county campaign in advocacy of its ratification. In this election the Democrats pursued a course that was just the opposite of that pursued by them in the election of delegates to the

Constitutional Convention. They decided that it was no longer unwise and dangerous for white men to take part in an election in which colored men were allowed to participate. This was due largely to the fact that the work of the convention had been far different from what they had anticipated. The newly framed Constitution was, taken as a whole, such an excellent document that in all probability it would have been ratified without serious opposition but for the fact that there was an unfortunate, unwise and unnecessary clause in it which practically disfranchised those who had held an office under the Constitution of the United States and who, having taken an oath to support and defend the Constitution of the United States, had afterwards supported the cause of the Confederacy. This clause caused very bitter and intense opposition to the ratification of the Constitution. When the election was over it was found that the Constitution had been rejected by a small majority. This result could not be fairly accepted as an indication of the strength of the two parties in the State, for it was a well-known fact that the Republican party had a clear majority of about 30,000.

Notwithstanding the large Republican majority in the State, which was believed to be safe, sure and reliable, there were several causes that contributed to the rejection of the newly framed Constitution. Among the causes were:

First. In consequence of the bitterness with which the ratification of the Constitution had been fought, on account of the objectionable clause referred to, intimidating methods had been adopted in several counties in which there was a large colored vote, resulting in a loss of several thousand votes for the Constitution.

Second. There were several thousand Republicans both white and colored,— but chiefly colored, — who were opposed to that offensive and objectionable clause, believing the same to be unjust, unnecessary, and unwise; hence, many of that class refused to vote either way.

Third. There were thousands of voters, the writer being one of that number, who favored ratification because the Constitution as a whole was a most excellent document, and because its ratification would facilitate the readmittance of Mississippi into the Union; after which the one objectionable clause could be stricken out by means of an amendment. While all of this class favored and advocated ratification for the reasons stated, yet their known attitude towards the clause proved to be a contributary cause of the rejection of the Constitution.

The reader may not understand why there were any colored men, especially at that time and in that section, that would have any sympathy for the white men who would have been victims of this clause had the new Constitution been ratified. But if the reader will closely follow what this writer will set down in subsequent chapters of this work, he will find the reasons why there was and still is a bond of sympathy between the two races at the South,— a bond that the institution of slavery with all its horrors could not destroy, the Rebellion could not wipe out, Reconstruction could not efface, and subsequent events have not been able to change. The writer is aware of the fact that thousands of intelligent people are now laboring under the impression that there exists at the South a bitter feeling of antagonism between the two races and that this has produced dangerous and difficult problems for the country to solve. That some things have occurred that would justify such a conclusion, especially on the part of those who are not students of this subject, will not be denied.

After the rejection of the Constitution no further effort was made to have Mississippi readmitted into the Union until after the Presidential and Congressional elections of 1868. The Democratic party throughout the country was solid in its support of President Andrew Johnson, and was bitter in its opposition to the Congressional Plan of Reconstruction. Upon a platform that declared the Reconstruction Acts of Congress to be unconstitutional, revolutionary, and void, the Democrats nominated for President and Vice-President, Ex-Governor Horatio Seymour, of New York, and General Frank P. Blair, of Missouri. The Republicans nominated for President General U. S. Grant, of Illinois, and for Vice-President Speaker Schuyler Colfax, of Indiana. These candidates were nominated upon a platform which strongly supported and indorsed the Congressional Plan of Reconstruction.

On this issue the two parties went before the people for a decision. The Republicans were successful, but not by such a decisive majority as in the Congressional election of 1866. In fact, if all the Southern States that took part in that election had gone Democratic, the hero of Appomattox would have been defeated. It was the Southern States, giving Republican majorities through the votes of their colored men, that saved that important national election to the Republican party. To the very great surprise of the Republican leaders the party lost the important and pivotal State of New York. It had been confidently believed that the immense popularity of General Grant and his prestige as a brilliant and successful Union general would save every doubtful State to the Republicans, New York, of course, included. But this expectation was not realized. The result, it is needless to say, was a keen and bitter disappointment, for no effort had been spared to bring to the attention of the voters the strong points in General Grant. A vote against Grant, it was strongly contended, was virtually a vote against the Union. Frederick Douglass, who electrified many audiences in that campaign, made the notable declaration that " While Washington had given us a country, it was Grant who had saved us a country." And yet the savior of our country failed in that election to save to the Republican party the most important State in the Union. But, notwithstanding the loss of New York, the Republicans not only elected the President and Vice-President, but also had a safe majority in both branches of Congress.

One of the first acts of Congress after the Presidential election of 1868 was one authorizing the President to submit Mississippi's rejected Constitution once again to a popular vote. The same act authorized the President to submit to a separate vote such clause or clauses of said Constitution as in his judgment might be particularly obnoxious to any considerable number of the people of the State. It was not and could not be denied that the Constitution as a whole was a most admirable document. The Democrats had no serious objection to its ratification if the clause disfranchising most of their leaders were eliminated. When it became known that this clause would be submitted to a separate vote, and that the Republican organization would not insist upon its retention, no serious opposition

to the ratification of the Constitution was anticipated. And, indeed, none was made.

The time fixed for holding the election was
November, 1869. In the mean time the State was
to be under military control. General Adelbert
Ames was made Military Governor, with power to
fill by appointment every civil office in the State.
Shortly after General Ames took charge as Military
Governor the Republican club at Natchez agreed
upon a slate to be submitted to the Military Governor for his favorable consideration, the names upon
said slate being the choice of the Republican organization of the county for county and city officials.
Among the names thus agreed upon was that of the
Rev. H. P. Jacobs for Justice of the Peace. It was
then decided to send a member of the club to Jackson, the State capital, to present the slate to the
Governor in person in order to answer questions
that might be asked or to give any information
that might be desired about any of the persons
whose names appeared on the slate. It fell to my
lot to be chosen for that purpose; the necessary
funds being raised by the club to pay my expenses.
I accepted the mission, contingent upon my employer's granting me leave of absence.

Natchez at that time was not connected with
Jackson by railroad, so that the only way for me to
reach the capital was to go by steamer from Natchez
to Vicksburg or to New Orleans, and from there by

rail to Jackson. The trip, therefore, would necessarily consume the greater part of a week. My
employer,— who was what was known as a Northern man, having come there after the occupation of
the place by the Federal troops,— not only granted
me leave of absence but agreed to remain in the city
and carry on the business during my absence.

When I arrived at the building occupied by the
Governor and sent up my card, I had to wait only
a few minutes before I was admitted to his office.
The Governor received me cordially and treated me
with marked courtesy, giving close attention while I
presented as forcibly as I could the merits and qualifications of the different persons whose names were
on the slate. When I had concluded my remarks
the Governor's only reply was that he would give
the matter his early and careful consideration. A
few weeks later the appointments were announced;
but not many of the appointees were persons whose
names I had presented. However, to my great embarrassment I found that my own name had been
substituted for that of Jacobs for the office of Justice of the Peace. I not only had no ambition in that
direction but was not aware that my name was
under consideration for that or for any other office.
Besides, I was apprehensive that Jacobs and some
of his friends might suspect me of having been false
to the trust that had been reposed in me, at least so
far as the office of Justice of the Peace was con-

cerned. At first I was of the opinion that the only way in which I could disabuse their minds of that erroneous impression was to decline the appointment. But I found out upon inquiry that in no event would Jacobs receive the appointment. I was also reliably informed that I had not been recommended nor suggested by any one, but that the Governor's action was the result of the favorable impression I had made upon him when I presented the slate. For this, of course, I was in no way responsible. In fact the impression of my fitness for the office that my brief talk had made upon the Governor was just what the club had hoped I would be able to accomplish in the interest of the whole slate. That it so happened that I was the beneficiary of the favorable impression that my brief talk had made upon the Governor may have been unfortunate in one respect, but it was an unconscious act for which I could not be censured. After consulting, therefore, with a few personal friends and local party leaders, I decided to accept the appointment although, in consequence of my youth and inexperience, I had serious doubts as to my ability to discharge the duties of the office which at that time was one of considerable importance.

Then the bond question loomed up, which was one of the greatest obstacles in my way, although the amount was only two thousand dollars. How to give that bond was the important problem I had to solve, for, of course, no one was eligible as a bondsman who did not own real estate. There were very few colored men who were thus eligible, and it was out of the question at that time to expect any white property owner to sign the bond of a colored man. But there were two colored men willing to sign the bond for one thousand dollars each who were considered eligible by the authorities. These men were William McCary and David Singleton. The law, having been duly satisfied in the matter of my bond, I was permitted to take the oath of office in April, 1869, and to enter upon the discharge of my duties as a Justice of the Peace, which office I held until the 31st of December of the same year when I resigned to accept a seat in the lower branch of the State Legislature to which I had been elected the preceding November.

When I entered upon the discharge of my duties as a Justice of the Peace the only comment that was made by the local Democratic paper of the town was in these words: " We are now beginning to reap the ravishing fruits of Reconstruction."

CHAPTER II

The new Constitution of Mississippi, which had been rejected in 1868, was to be submitted to a popular vote once more in November, 1869. At the same time State officers, members of the Legislature, Congressmen, and district and county officers were to be elected. Since the objectionable clauses in the Constitution were to be put to a separate vote, and since it was understood that both parties would favor the rejection of these clauses, there was no serious opposition to the ratification of the Constitution thus amended. A hard and stubborn fight was, however, to be made for control of the State Government.

General James L. Alcorn, who had been a general in the Confederate Army and who had recently openly identified himself with the Republican party, was nominated by the Republicans for the office of Governor of the State. Of the other six men who were associated with him on the state ticket, only the candidate for Secretary of the State, the Reverend James Lynch,— an able and eloquent minister of the Methodist Church,— was a colored man. Lynch was a man of fine ability, of splendid education, and one of the most powerful and convincing orators that the Republicans had upon the stump in that campaign. He was known and recognized as such an able and brilliant speaker that his services were in great demand from the beginning to the end of the campaign. No Democratic orator, however able, was anxious to meet him in joint debate. He died suddenly the latter part of 1872. His death was a great loss to the State and to the Republican party and especially to the colored race.

Of the other five candidates on the ticket two,— the candidates for State Treasurer and Attorney General,— were, like General Alcorn, Southern white men. The candidate for State Treasurer, Hon. W. H. Vasser, was a successful business man who lived in the northern part of the State, while the candidate for Attorney General, Hon. Joshua S. Morris, was a brilliant member of the bar who lived in the southern part of the State. The other three, the candidates for Lieutenant-Governor, State Auditor and Superintendent of Education, were Northern men who had settled in the State after the War, called by the Democrats, "Carpet Baggers," but they were admitted to be clean and good men who had lived in the State long enough to become fully identified with its industrial and business interests. H. C. Powers, the candidate for Lieutenant-

Governor, and H. Musgrove, the candidate for Auditor of Public Accounts, were successful cotton planters from Noxubee and Clarke counties respectively; while H. R. Pease, the candidate for State Superintendent of Education, had been identified with educational work ever since he came to the State. It could not be denied that it was a strong and able ticket,— one that the Democrats would find it very difficult to defeat. In desperation the Democratic party had nominated as their candidate for Governor a brother-in-law of President Grant's, Judge Lewis Dent, in the hope that the President would throw the weight of his influence and the active support of his administration on the side of his relative, as against the candidate of his own party, especially in view of the fact that Dent had been nominated not as a Democrat but as an Independent Republican,— his candidacy simply having been indorsed by the Democratic organization. But in this they were disappointed, for if the President gave any indication of preference it was in favor of the Republican ticket. General Ames, for instance, was the Military Governor of the State, holding that position at the pleasure of the President; and Ames was so outspoken in his support of the Republican ticket, that in an address before the State Republican Convention that nominated General Alcorn for the Governorship he announced, " You have my sympathy and shall have my support." This declaration was received by the convention with great applause, for it was known that those words from that source carried great weight. They meant not only that the Republican party would have the active and aggressive support of the Military Governor,— which was very important and would be worth thousands of votes to the party,— but they also indicated the attitude of the National Administration. The campaign was aggressive from beginning to end. Judge Dent was at a disadvantage, since his candidacy had failed to bring to his support the influence of the National Administration, which had been the sole purpose of his nomination. In spite of that fact Dent made a game and gallant fight; but the election resulted in an overwhelming Republican victory. That party not only elected the State ticket by a majority of about 30,000 but it also had a large majority in both branches of the State Legislature.

The new administration had an important and difficult task before it. A State Government had to be organized from top to bottom; a new judiciary had to be inaugurated,— consisting of three Justices of the State Supreme Court, fifteen Judges of the Circuit Court and twenty Chancery Court Judges,— who had all to be appointed by the Governor with the consent of the Senate, and, in addition, a new public school system had to be established. There was not a public school building anywhere in the

State except in a few of the larger towns, and they, with possibly a few exceptions, were greatly in need of repairs. To erect the necessary school houses and to reconstruct and repair those already in existence so as to afford educational facilities for both races was by no means an easy task. It necessitated a very large outlay of cash in the beginning, which resulted in a material increase in the rate of taxation for the time being, but the Constitution called for the establishment of the system, and of course the work had to be done. It was not only done, but it was done creditably and as economically as possible, considering the conditions at that time. That system, though slightly changed, still stands,— a creditable monument to the first Republican State administration that was organized in the State of Mississippi under the Reconstruction Acts of Congress.

It was also necessary to reorganize, reconstruct and, in many instances, rebuild some of the penal and charitable institutions of the State. A new code of laws also had to be adopted to take the place of the old code and thus wipe out the black laws that had been passed by what was known as the Johnson Legislature and in addition bring about other changes so as to make the laws and statutes of the State conform with the new order of things. This was no easy task, in view of the fact that a heavy increase in the rate of taxation was thus made necessary, for the time being at least. That this important work was splendidly, creditably, and economically done no fair-minded person who is familiar with the facts will question or dispute.

That the State never had before, and has never had since, a finer Judiciary than that which was organized under the administration of Governor Alcorn and which continued under the administration of Governor Ames is an indisputable and incontrovertible fact. The Judges of the Supreme Court were E. G. Peyton, H. F. Simrall and J. Tarbell, who in Mississippi had no superiors in their profession, and who had the respect and confidence of the bar and of the people without regard to race or politics. Judge Peyton was the Chief Justice, Simrall and Tarbell being the Associate Justices. The first two were old residents of the State, while Mr. Justice Tarbell was what the Democrats would call a " Carpet Bagger." But that he was an able lawyer and a man of unimpeachable integrity no one doubted or questioned. During the second administration of President Grant he held the important position of Second Comptroller of the United States Treasury. The Circuit Court bench was graced with such able and brilliant lawyers as Jason Niles, G. C. Chandler, George F. Brown, J. A. Orr, John W. Vance, Robert Leachman, B. B. Boone, Orlando Davis, James M. Smiley, Uriah Millsaps, William M. Hancock, E. S. Fisher, C. C.

Shackleford, W. B. Cunningham, W. D. Bradford and A. Alderson. Judges Brown and Cunningham were the only ones in the above list who were not old residents of the State. After leaving the bench, Judge Chandler served for several years as United States Attorney. Judge Niles served one term as a member of Congress, having been elected as a Republican in 1875. His son Henry Clay Niles is now United States District Judge for the State, having been appointed to that important position by President Harrison. He was strongly recommended by many members of the bench and bar of the State; and the very able and creditable way in which he has discharged the duties of the position has more than demonstrated the wisdom of the selection.

The Chancery Courts as organized by Governor Alcorn and continued by Governor Ames were composed of men no less able and brilliant than those who composed the Bench of the Circuit Courts. They were: J. C. Lyon, E. P. Harmon, E. G. Peyton, Jr., J. M. Ellis, G. S. McMillan, Samuel Young, W. G. Henderson, Edwin Hill, T. R. Gowan, J. F. Simmons, Wesley Drane, D. W. Walker, DeWitte Stearns, D. P. Coffee, E. W. Cabiness, A. E. Reynolds, Thomas Christian, Austin Pollard, J. J. Hooker, O. H. Whitfield, E. Stafford, W. A. Drennan, Thomas Walton, E. H. Osgood, C. A. Sullivan, Hiram Cassedy, Jr., W. B.

Peyton, J. D. Barton, J. J. Dennis, W. D. Frazee, P. P. Bailey, L. C. Abbott, H. W. Warren, R. Boyd, R. B. Stone, William Breck, J. N. Campbell, H. R. Ware and J. B. Deason. The above names composed those who were appointed both by Governors Alcorn and Ames. A majority of those originally appointed by Governor Alcorn were reappointed by Governor Ames. Of the forty appointments of Judges of the Chancery Courts made under the administrations of Alcorn and Ames, not more than about seven were not to the " manner born." The administration of James L. Alcorn as Governor of the State of Mississippi is one of the best with which that unfortunate State has been blessed. A more extended reference to the subsequent administration of Governor Ames will be made in a later chapter.

CHAPTER III

Although it was not charged nor even intimated that my acceptance of the office of Justice of the Peace was the result of bad faith on my part, still the appointment resulted in the creation for the time being of two factions in the Republican party in the county. One was known as the Lynch faction, the other as the Jacobs faction.

When the Constitution was submitted to a popular vote in November, 1869, it was provided that officers should be elected at the same time to all offices created by the Constitution and that they, including members of the Legislature, were to be chosen by popular vote. The county of Adams (Natchez) was entitled to one member of the State Senate and three members of the House of Representatives. Jacobs was a candidate for the Republican nomination for State Senator. The Lynch faction, however, refused to support him for that position although it had no objection to his nomination for member of the House. Since Jacobs persisted in his candidacy for State Senator the Lynch faction brought out an opposing candidate in the person of a Baptist minister by the name of J. M. P. Williams. The contest between the two Republican candidates was interesting and exciting, though not bitter, and turned out to be very close.

The convention was to be composed of thirty-three delegates, seventeen being necessary to nominate. The result at the primary election of delegates to the convention was so close that it was impossible to tell which one had a majority, since there were several delegates,— about whose attitude and preference there had been some doubt, — who refused to commit themselves either way. In the organization of the convention the Williams men gained the first advantage, one of their number having been made permanent chairman. But this was not important since there were no contests for seats, consequently the presiding officer would have no occasion to render a decision that could have any bearing upon the composition of the body over which he presided.

Both sides agreed that the nomination for State Senator should be made first and that the vote should be by ballot, the ballots to be received and counted by two tellers, one to be selected by each faction. When the result of the first ballot was announced, Jacobs had sixteen votes, Williams, sixteen, and a third man had one. Several ballots were taken with the same result, when, with the consent of both sides, a recess was taken until 3 o'clock in the afternoon. The one delegate that refused to vote for either Jacobs or Williams made no effort to conceal his identity. To the contrary, he was outspoken in his determination and decision that he would not at any time or under any circumstances vote for either. Strange to say, this man was also a colored Baptist preacher, the Rev. Noah Buchanan, from the Washington district. Members of both factions approached him during the recess and pleaded with him, but their efforts and pleadings were all in vain. Nothing could move him or change him. He stated that he had given the matter his careful and serious consideration, and that he had come to the conclusion that neither Jacobs nor Williams was a fit man to represent the important county of Adams in the State Senate, hence neither could get his vote. At the afternoon session, after several ballots had been taken with the same result, an adjournment was ordered until 9 o'clock next morning.

Soon after adjournment each side went into caucus. At the Jacobs meeting it was decided to stick to their man to the very last. At the Williams meeting Hon. H. C. Griffin, white leader of the Williams men, suggested the name of the Rev. H. R. Revels as a compromise candidate. Revels was comparatively a new man in the community. He had recently been stationed at Natchez as pastor in charge of the A. M. E. Church, and so far as known he had never voted, had never attended a political meeting, and of course, had never made a political speech. But he was a colored man, and presumed to be a Republican, and believed to be a man of ability and considerably above the average in point of intelligence; just the man, it was thought, the Rev. Noah Buchanan would be willing to vote for.

After considerable discussion it was agreed that a committee should be appointed to wait on Mr. Williams in order to find out if he would be willing to withdraw in favor of Revels should his friends and supporters deem such a step necessary and wise. In the event of Williams' withdrawal, the committee was next to call on Revels to find out if he would consent to the use of his name. If Revels consented, the committee was next to call on Rev. Buchanan to find out whether or not he would vote for Revels. This committee was to report to the caucus at 8 o'clock next morning.

At the appointed time the committee reported that Williams had stated that he was in the hands of his friends and that he would abide by any decision they might make. Revels, the report stated, who had been taken very much by surprise,— having had no idea that his name would ever be mentioned in connection with any office,— had asked to be allowed until 7 o'clock in the morning to consider the matter and to talk it over with his wife. At

7 o'clock he notified the chairman of the committee that he would accept the nomination if tendered.

Buchanan had informed the committee that he had heard of Revels but did not know him personally. He too had asked to be allowed until 7 o'clock in the morning before giving a positive answer, so as to enable him to make the necessary inquiries to find out whether or not Revels was a suitable man for the position. At 7 o'clock he informed the chairman of the committee that if the name of Williams should be withdrawn in favor of Revels he would cast his vote for Revels. The caucus then decided by a unanimous vote that upon the assembling of the convention at 9 o'clock that morning Mr. Griffin should withdraw the name of Williams from before the convention as a candidate for State Senator, but that no other name should be placed in nomination. Every member of the caucus, however, was committed to vote for Revels. This decision was to be communicated to no one outside of the caucus except to Mr. Buchanan, who was to be privately informed of it by the chairman of the committee to whom he had communicated his own decision.

As soon as the convention was called to order Mr. Griffin was recognized by the chair. He stated that he had been authorized to withdraw the name of Rev. J. M. P. Williams from before the convention as candidate for State Senator. This announcement was received by the Jacobs men with great applause. The withdrawal of the name of Williams without placing any other in nomination they accepted as evidence that further opposition to the nomination of their candidate had been abandoned and that his nomination was a foregone conclusion. But they were not allowed to labor under that impression very long. The roll-call was immediately ordered by the chair and the tellers took their places. When the ballots had been counted and tabulated, the result was seventeen votes for Revels and sixteen votes for Jacobs. The announcement was received by the Williams men with great applause. The result was a victory for them because it was their sixteen votes together with the vote of Rev. Noah Buchanan that had nominated Revels. The Jacobs men accepted their defeat gracefully. A motion was offered by their leader to make the nomination unanimous and it was adopted without a dissenting vote. In anticipation of his nomination Revels was present as one of the interested spectators and upon being called upon for a brief address he delivered it with telling effect, thereby making a most favorable impression. This address convinced Rev. Noah Buchanan that he had made no mistake in voting for Revels. Jacobs was then nominated for member of the House of Representatives without opposition, his associates being John R. Lynch and Capt. O. C. French, a white Republican. The ticket as completed was elected by a majority of from fifteen hundred to two thousand, a Republican nomination in Adams County at that time being equivalent to an election.

When the Legislature convened at Jackson the first Monday in January, 1870, it was suggested to Lieutenant-Governor Powers, presiding officer of the Senate, that he invite the Rev. Dr. Revels to open the Senate with prayer. The suggestion was favorably acted upon. That prayer,— one of the most impressive and eloquent prayers that had ever been delivered in the Senate Chamber,— made Revels a United States Senator. He made a profound impression upon all who heard him. It impressed those who heard it that Revels was not only a man of great natural ability but that he was also a man of superior attainments.

The duty devolved upon that Legislature to fill three vacancies in the United States Senate: one, a fractional term of about one year,— the remainder of the six year term to which Jefferson Davis had been elected before the breaking out of the Rebellion,— another fractional term of about five years, and the third, the full term of six years, beginning with the expiration of the fractional term of one year. The colored members of the Legislature constituted a very small minority not only of the total membership of that body but also of the Republican members. Of the thirty-three members of which the Senate was composed four of them were colored men: H. R. Revels, of Adams; Charles Caldwell, of Hinds; Robert Gleed, of Lowndes, and T. W. Stringer, of Warren. Of the one hundred and seven members of which the House was composed about thirty of them were colored men. It will thus be seen that out of the one hundred forty members of which the two Houses were composed only about thirty-four of them were colored men. But the colored members insisted that one of the three United States Senators to be elected should be a colored man. The white Republicans were willing that the colored men be given the fractional term of one year, since it was understood that Governor Alcorn was to be elected to the full term of six years and that Governor Ames was to be elected to the fractional term of five years.

In this connection it may not be out of place to say that, ever since the organization of the Republican party in Mississippi, the white Republicans of that State, unlike some in a few of the other Southern States, have never attempted to draw the color line against their colored allies. In this they have proved themselves to be genuine and not sham Republicans,— that is to say, Republicans from principle and conviction and not for plunder and spoils. They have never failed to recognize the fact that the fundamental principle of the Republican party,

— the one that gave the party its strongest claim upon the confidence and support of the public,— is its advocacy of equal civil and political rights. If that party should ever come to the conclusion that this principle should be abandoned, that moment it will merit, and I am sure it will receive, the condemnation and repudiation of the public.

It was not, therefore, a surprise to any one when the white Republican members of the Mississippi Legislature gave expression to their entire willingness to vote for a suitable colored man to represent the state of Mississippi in the highest and most dignified legislative tribunal in the world. The next step was to find the man. The name of the Rev. James Lynch was first suggested. That he was a suitable and fit man for the position could not be denied. But he had just been elected Secretary of State for a term of four years, and his election to the Senate would have created a vacancy in the former office which would have necessitated the holding of another State election and another election was what all wanted to avoid. For that reason his name was not seriously considered for the Senatorship.

The next name suggested was that of the Rev. H. R. Revels and those who had been so fortunate as to hear the impressive prayer that he had delivered on the opening of the Senate were outspoken in their advocacy of his selection. The white Re-

HON. HIRAM R. REVELS.
The first colored man that occupied a seat in the
U. S. Senate. From a photograph taken by Maj.
Lynch at Natchez, Miss., in 1868.

publicans assured the colored members that if they would unite upon Revels, they were satisfied he would receive the vote of every white Republican member of the Legislature. Governor Alcorn also gave the movement his cordial and active support, thus insuring for Revels the support of the State administration. The colored members then held an informal conference, at which it was unanimously decided to present the name of Rev. H. R. Revels to the Republican Legislative Caucus as a candidate for United States Senator to fill the fractional term of one year. The choice was ratified by the caucus without serious opposition. In the joint Legislative session, every Republican member, white and colored, voted for the three Republican caucus nominees for United States Senators,— Alcorn, Ames and Revels,— with one exception, Senator William M. Hancock, of Lauderdale, who stated in explanation of his vote against Revels that as a lawyer he did not believe that a colored man was eligible to a seat in the United States Senate. But Judge Hancock seems to have been the only lawyer in the Legislature,— or outside of it, as far as could be learned,— who entertained that opinion.

CHAPTER IV

In addition to the election of three United States
Senators this Legislature had some very important
work before it, as has already been stated in a previous chapter. A new public school system had to be
inaugurated and put in operation, thus necessitating
the construction of schoolhouses throughout the
State, some of them, especially in the towns and
villages, to be quite large and of course expensive.
All of the other public buildings and institutions in
the State had to be repaired, some of them rebuilt,
all of them having been neglected and some of them
destroyed during the progress of the late War. In
addition to this the entire State Government in all
of its branches had to be reconstructed and so organized as to place the same in perfect harmony
with the new order of things.

To accomplish these things money was required.
There was none in the treasury. There was no
cash available even to pay the ordinary expenses
of the State government. Because of this lack of
funds the government had to be carried on on a

credit basis,— that is, by the issuing of notes or warrants based upon the credit of the State. These notes were issued at par to the creditors of the State in satisfaction of the obligations. In turn they were disposed of at a discount to bankers and brokers by whom they were held until there should be sufficient cash in the treasury to redeem them,— such redemption usually occurring in from three to six months, though sometimes the period was longer. To raise the necessary money to put the new machinery in successful operation one of two things had to be done: either the rate of taxation must be materially increased or interest bearing bonds must be issued and placed upon the market, thus increasing the bonded debt of the State. Although the fact was subsequently developed that a small increase in the bonded debt of the State could not very well be avoided, yet, after careful deliberation, the plan agreed upon was to materially increase the rate of taxation.

This proved to be so unpopular that it came near losing the Legislature to the Republicans at the elections of 1871. Although it was explained to the people that this increase was only temporary and that the rate of taxation would be reduced as soon as some of the schoolhouses had been built, and some of the public institutions had been repaired, still this was not satisfactory to those by whom these taxes had to be paid. They insisted that some other plan ought to have been adopted, especially at that time. The War had just come to a close, leaving most of the people in an impoverished condition. What was true of the public institutions of the State was equally true of the private property of those who were property owners at that time. Their property during the War had been neglected, and what had not been destroyed was in a state of decay. This was especially true of those who had been the owners of large landed estates and of many slaves. Many of these people had been the acknowledged representatives of the wealth, the intelligence, the culture, the refinement and the aristocracy of the South,— the ruling class in the church, in society and in State affairs. These were the men who had made and molded public opinion, who had controlled the pulpit and the press, who had shaped the destiny of the State; who had made and enforced the laws,— or at least such laws as they desired to have enforced,— and who had represented the State not only in the State Legislature but in both branches of the National Legislature at Washington. Many of these proud sons, gallant fathers, cultured mothers and wives and refined and polished daughters found themselves in a situation and in a condition that was pitiable in the extreme. It was not only a difficult matter for them to adjust themselves to the new order of things and to the radically changed conditions, but no longer having slaves upon whom they could depend for everything, to raise the necessary money to prevent the decay, the dissipation and the ultimate loss or destruction of their large landed estates was the serious and difficult problem they had before them. To have the rate of taxation increased upon this property, especially at that particular time, was to them a very serious matter,— a matter which could not have any other effect than to intensify their bitterness and hostility towards the party in control of the State Government. But since Governor Alcorn, under whose administration, and in accordance with whose recommendation this increase had been made, was a typical representative of this particular class, it was believed and hoped that he would have sufficient influence with the people of his own class to stem the tide of resentment, and to calm their fears and apprehensions. That the Republicans retained control of the Legislature as a result of the elections of 1871,— though by only a small majority in the lower house,— is conclusive evidence that the Governor's efforts in that direction were not wholly in vain. The argument made by the taxpayers, however, was plausible and it may be conceded that, upon the whole, they were about right; for no doubt it would have been much easier upon the taxpayers to have increased at that time the interest-bearing debt of the State than to have increased the tax rate. The latter course, however, had been adopted and could not then be changed.

Governor Alcorn also recommended,— a recommendation that was favorably considered by the Legislature,— that there be created and supported by the State a college for the higher education of the colored boys and young men of the State. This bill was promptly passed by the Legislature, and, in honor of the one by whom its creation was recommended the institution was named " Alcorn College." The presidency of this much-needed college was an honorable and dignified position to which a fair and reasonable salary was attached, so the Governor, who had the appointing power, decided to tender the office to Senator H. R. Revels upon the expiration of his term in the Senate. I had the honor of being named as one of the first trustees of this important institution. After the Governor, the trustees and Senator Revels had carefully inspected many different places that had been suggested for the location of the institution, Oakland College near the town of Rodney in Claiborne County, was finally purchased, and Alcorn College was established, with Senator Revels as its first president.

As an evidence of the necessity for such an institution it will not be out of place to call attention to the fact that when the writer was first elected to Congress in 1872, there was not one young colored man in the State that could pass the necessary examination for a clerkship in any of the Departments at Washington. Four years later the supply was greater than the demand, nearly all of the applicants being graduates of Alcorn College. At this writing the institution is still being maintained by the State, although on a reduced appropriation and on a plan that is somewhat different from that which was inaugurated at its beginning and while the Republicans were in control of the State government. One of the reasons, no doubt, why it is supported by a Democratic administration, is that the State might otherwise forfeit and lose the aid it now receives from the National Government for the support of agricultural institutions. But, aside from this, there are very many liberal, fairminded and influential Democrats in the State who are strongly in favor of having the State provide for the liberal education of both races.

The knowledge I had acquired of parliamentary law not only enabled me to take a leading part in the deliberations of the Legislature, but it resulted in my being made Speaker of the House of Representatives that was elected in 1871. Shortly after the adjournment of the first session of the Legislature, the Speaker of the House, Hon. F. E. Franklin, of Yazoo County, died. When the Legislature reassembled the first Monday in January, 1871,

Hon. H. W. Warren, of Leake County, was made Speaker of the House. In addition to the vacancy from Yazoo, created by the death of Speaker Franklin, one had also occurred from Lowndes County, which was one of the safe and sure Republican counties. Through apathy, indifference and overconfidence, the Democratic candidate, Dr. Landrum, was elected to fill this vacancy. It was a strange and novel sight to see a Democratic member of the Legislature from the rock-ribbed Republican county of Lowndes. It was no doubt a source of considerable embarrassment even to Dr. Landrum himself, for he was looked upon by all as a marvel and a curiosity. When he got up to deliver his maiden speech a few days after he was sworn in, he was visibly and perceptibly affected, for every eye was firmly and intently fixed upon him. Every one seemed to think that the man that could be elected to a seat in the Legislature from Lowndes County as a Democrat, must be endowed with some strange and hidden power through the exercise of which he could direct the movements and control the actions of those who might be brought in contact with him or subjected to his hypnotic influence; hence the anxiety and curiosity to hear the maiden speech of this strange and remarkable man. The voice in the House of a Democrat from the county of Lowndes was of so strange, so sudden, so unexpected and so remarkable that it was difficult for many to bring themselves to a realization of the fact that such a thing had actually happened and that it was a living reality. To the curious, the speech was a disappointment, although it was a plain, calm, conservative and convincing statement of the new member's position upon public questions. To the great amusement of those who heard him he related some of his experiences while he was engaged in canvassing the county. But the speech revealed the fact that, after all, he was nothing more than an ordinary man. No one was impressed by any word or sentence that had fallen from his lips that there was anything about him that was strange, impressive or unusual, and all decided that his election was purely accidental; for it was no more surprising than was the election of a colored Republican, Hon. J. M. Wilson, to the same Legislature the year before, from the reliable Democratic county of Marion.

There was not much to be done at the second session of the Legislature outside of passing the annual appropriation bills; hence the session was a short one. Although Governor Alcorn's term as a United States Senator commenced March 4, 1871, he did not vacate the office of Governor until the meeting of Congress, the first Monday in the following December. A new Legislature and all county officers were to be elected in November of that year. It was to be the first important election since the inauguration of the Alcorn administration. The Governor decided to remain where he could assume entire responsibility for what had been done and where he could answer, officially and otherwise, all charges and accusations and criticisms that might be made against his administration and his official acts. The Republican majority in the State Senate was so large that the holdover Senators made it well nigh impossible for the Democrats to secure a majority of that body, but the principal fight was to be made for control of the House. As already stated the heavy increase in taxation proved to be very unpopular and this gave the Democrats a decided advantage. They made a strong and bitter fight to gain control of the House, and nearly succeeded.

When every county had been heard from it was found that out of the one hundred fifteen members of which the House was composed, the Republicans had elected sixty-six members and the Democrats, forty-nine. Of the sixty-six that had been elected as Republicans, two,—Messrs. Armstead and Streeter,—had been elected from Carroll County on an independent ticket. They classed themselves politically as Independent or Alcorn Republicans. Carroll was the only doubtful county in the State that the Democrats failed to carry. The Independent ticket in that county, which was supported by an influential faction of Democrats, was brought out with the understanding and agreement that it would receive the support of the Republican organization. This support was given, but upon a pledge that the candidates for the Legislature, if elected, should not enter the Democratic caucus, nor vote for the candidates thereof in the organization of the House. These conditions were accepted, which resulted in the ticket being supported by the Republicans and, consequently elected. All the other doubtful and close counties went Democratic, which resulted in the defeat of some of the strongest and most influential men in the Republican party, including Speaker Warren of Leake County, Lucas and Boyd of Altala, Underwood of Chickasaw, Avery of Tallahatchie, and many others. Notwithstanding these reverses, the Republicans sent a number of able men to the House, among whom may be mentioned French of Adams, Howe and Pyles of Panola, Fisher of Hinds, Chandler and Davis of Noxubee, Huggins of Monroe, Stone and Spelman of Madison, Barrett of Amite, Sullivan and Gayles of Bolivar, Everett and Dixon of Yazoo, Griggs and Houston of Issaquina, and many others. In point of experience and ability this Legislature was the equal of its immediate predecessor.

CHAPTER V

The elections being over, and a Republican majority in both branches of the Legislature being assured, Governor Alcorn was then prepared to vacate the office of Governor, to turn over the administration of State affairs to Lieutenant-Governor Powers and to proceed to Washington so as to be present at the opening session of Congress on the first Monday in December when he would assume his duties as a United States Senator.

The Legislature was to meet the first Monday in the following January,— 1872. As soon as the fact was made known that the Republicans would control the organization of the House, the Speakership of that body began to be agitated. If Speaker Warren had been reëlected he would have received the Republican caucus nomination without opposition, but his defeat made it necessary for a new man to be brought forward for that position. A movement was immediately put on foot to make me the Speaker of the House.

Upon a careful examination of the returns it

58

was found that of the one hundred fifteen members of which the House was composed there were seventy-seven whites and thirty-eight colored. Of the seventy-seven whites, forty-nine had been elected as Democrats and twenty-eight as Republicans. The thirty-eight colored men were all Republicans. It will thus be seen that, while in the composition of the Republican caucus there were ten more colored than white members, yet of the total membership of the House there were thirty-nine more white than colored members. But in the organization of the House, the contest was not between white and colored, but between Democrats and Republicans. No one had been elected,— at least on the Republican side,— because he was a white man or because he was a colored man, but because he was a Republican. After a preliminary canvass the fact was developed that the writer was not only the choice of the colored members for Speaker of the House, but of a large majority of the white Republican members as well. They believed,— and voted in accordance with that belief both in the party caucus and in the House,— that the writer was the best-equipped man for that responsible position. This fact had been demonstrated to their satisfaction during the two sessions of the preceding Legislature.

The nomination of the writer by the House Republican caucus for Speaker was a foregone conclusion several weeks before the convening of the Legislature. With a full membership in attendance fifty-eight votes would be necessary to perfect the organization. When the Republican caucus convened sixty members were present and took part in the deliberations thereof. Four of the Republicans-elect had not at that time arrived at the seat of government. The two Independents from Carroll refused to attend the caucus, but this did not necessarily mean that they would not vote for the candidates thereof in the organization of the House. But since we had sixty votes,— two more than were necessary to elect our candidate,— we believed that the organization would be easily perfected the next day, regardless of the action of the members from Carroll County.

In this, however, we were sadly disappointed. The result of the first vote for Speaker of the House was as follows:

> Lynch, Republican caucus nominee.. 55
> Streeter, Democratic nominee 47
> Chandler, Independent Republican .. 7
> Armstead, Independent Republican .. 1
> Howe, Regular Republican 1
> Necessary to elect 56

Judge Chandler of Noxubee, who had been elected as a regular Republican with four other white Republicans,— all of whom attended and took part in the caucus the night before,— refused to vote for the nominee of the caucus for Speaker but voted instead for Chandler. It will be seen that the vote for Streeter, the Democratic caucus nominee, was two less than that party's strength; thus showing that two Democrats must have also voted for Chandler. It will also be seen that if every vote that was not received by Lynch had been given to Chandler or to any other man, that man would have received the required number of votes and would have been elected. The Democrats stood ready to give their solid vote to any one of the Independents whenever it could be shown that their votes would result in an election. But it so happened that Chandler and Armstead were both ambitious to be Speaker and neither would give way for the other, which, of course, made the election of either impossible. The one vote cast for Howe was no doubt Mr. Armstead's vote, while the one vote for Armstead was no doubt cast by his colleague. In the nomination of Hon. H. M. Streeter, the Democrats selected their strongest man, and the best parliamentarian on their side of the House. The refusal of the so-called Independents to vote for the Republican caucus nominee for Speaker produced a deadlock which continued for a period of several days. At no time could any one of the regular Republicans be induced under any circumstances to vote for any one of the Independents.

They would much rather have the House organized by the Democrats than allow party treachery to be thus rewarded.

While the deadlock was in progress, Senators Alcorn and Ames suddenly made their appearance upon the scene of action. They had made the trip from Washington to use their influence to break the deadlock, and to bring about an organization of the House by the Republican party. But Senator Alcorn was the one that could render the most effective service in that direction, since the bolters were men who professed to be followers of his and loyal to his political interests and leadership.

As soon as the Senator arrived he held a conference with the bolters, including Messrs. Armstead and Streeter,— the two independents from Carroll. In addressing those who had been elected as Republicans and who had attended and participated in the caucus of that party, the Senator did not mince his words. He told them in plain language that they were in honor bound to support the caucus nominees of their party, or that they must resign their seats and allow their constituents to elect others that would do so. With reference to the Independents from Carroll, he said the situation was slightly different. They had been elected as Independents under conditions which did

not obligate them to enter the Republican caucus
or support the candidates thereof. They had
pledged themselves not to support the Democratic
caucus nominees, nor to aid that party in the organization of the House. Up to that time they
had not made a move, nor given a vote that could
be construed into a violation of the pledge under
which they had been elected, but they had publicly
declared on several occasions that they had been
elected as Independents or Alcorn Republicans. In
other words, they had been elected as friends and
supporters of the Alcorn administration, and of that
type of Republicanism for which he stood and of
which he was the representative. If this were true
then they should not hesitate to take the advice of
the man to support whose administration they had
been elected. He informed them that if they
meant what they said the best way for them to
prove it was to vote for the Republican caucus
nominees for officers of the House, because he was
the recognized leader of the party in the State and
that the issue involved in the elections was either
an endorsement or repudiation of his administration as Governor. Republican success under such
circumstances meant an endorsement of his administration, while Republican defeat would mean its
repudiation. The most effective way, then, in
which they could make good their ante-election

pledges and promises was to vote for the candidates of the Republican caucus for officers of the House.

The two Carroll County Independents informed the Senator that he had correctly outlined their position and their attitude, and that it was their purpose and their determination to give a loyal and effective support, so far as the same was in their power, to the policies and principles for which he stood and of which he was the accredited representative; but that they were apprehensive that they could not successfully defend their action and explain their votes to the satisfaction of their constituents if they were to vote for a colored man for Speaker of the House.

"But," said the Senator, "could you have been elected without the votes of colored men? If you now vote against a colored man,— who is in every way a fit and capable man for the position,— simply because he is a colored man, would you expect those men to support you in the future?"

The Senator also reminded them that they had received very many more colored than white votes; and that, in his opinion, very few of the white men who had supported them would find fault with them for voting for a capable and intelligent colored man to preside over the deliberations of the House.

"Can you then," the Senator asked, "afford to offend the great mass of colored men that supported you in order to please an insignificantly small number of narrow-minded whites?"

The Senator assured them that he was satisfied they had nothing to fear as a result of their action in voting for Mr. Lynch as Speaker of the House. He knew the candidate favorably and well and therefore did not hesitate to assure them that if they contributed to his election they would have no occasion to regret having done so. The conference then came to a close with the understanding that all present would vote the next day for the Republican caucus nominees for officers of the House. This was done. The result of the ballot the following day was as follows:

> Lynch, Republican caucus nominee, . 63
> Chandler, Independent Republican, .. 49
> Necessary to elect. 57

It will be seen that Judge Chandler received the solid Democratic vote while Lynch received the vote of every voting Republican present, including Chandler and the two Independents from Carroll, — three Republicans still being absent and not paired. By substantially the same vote ex-Speaker Warren, of Leake County, was elected Chief Clerk, and Ex-Representative Hill, of Marshall County, was elected Sergeant-at-arms. The Legislature was then organized and was ready to proceed to business.

At the conclusion of the session, the House not only adopted a resolution complimenting the Speaker and thanking him for the able and impartial manner in which he had presided over its deliberations, but presented him with a fine gold watch and chain,— purchased with money that had been contributed by members of both parties and by a few outside friends,— as a token of their esteem and appreciation of him as a presiding officer.   On the outside case of the watch these words were engraved: " Presented to Hon. J. R. Lynch, Speaker of the House of Representatives, by the Members of the Legislature, April 19, 1873."   That watch the writer still has and will keep as a sacred family heirloom.

A good deal of work was to be done by this Legislature.   The seats of a number of Democrats were contested.   But the decision in many cases was in favor of the sitting members.   The changes, however, were sufficient to materially increase the Republican majority.

Among the important bills to be passed was one to divide the State into six Congressional Districts. The apportionment of Representatives in Congress, under the Apportionment Act which had recently passed Congress, increased the number of Representatives from Mississippi, which had formerly been five, to six.   Republican leaders in both branches of the Legislature decided that the duty of drawing up a bill apportioning the State into Congressional Districts should devolve upon the Speaker of the House, with the understanding that the party organization would support the bill drawn by him.

I accepted the responsibility, and immediately proceeded with the work of drafting a bill for that purpose. Two plans had been discussed, each of which had strong supporters and advocates. One plan was so to apportion the State as to make all of the districts Republican; but in doing so the majority in at least two of the districts would be quite small. The other was so to apportion the State as to make five districts safely and reliably Republican and the remaining one Democratic. I had not taken a decided stand for or against either plan. Perhaps that was one reason why the advocates of both plans agreed to refer the matter to me for a final decision.

The Democrats heard what had been done. One of them, Hon. F. M. Goar, of Lee County, called to see me so as to talk over the matter. He expressed the hope that in drawing up the bill, one district would be conceded to the Democrats.

"If this is done," he said, "I assume that the group of counties located in the northeastern part of the State will be the Democratic district. In that event we will send a very strong and able man to Congress in the person of Hon. L. Q. C. Lamar."

I had every reason to believe that if Mr. Lamar were sent to Congress he would reflect credit upon himself, his party, and his State. I promised to give the suggestion earnest and perhaps favorable consideration. After going over the matter carefully I came to the conclusion that the better and safer plan would be to make five safe and sure Republican districts and concede one to the Democrats. Another reason for this decision was that in so doing, the State could be more fairly apportioned. The Republican counties could be easily made contiguous and the population in each district could be made as nearly equal as possible. The apportionment could not have been so fairly and equitably made if the other plan had been adopted.

After the bill had been completed, it was submitted to a joint caucus of the Republican members of the two Houses, and after a brief explanation by me of its provisions it was accepted and approved by the unanimous vote of the caucus. When it was brought before the house, a majority of the Democratic members,— under the leadership of Messrs. Streeter, Roane and McIntosh,— fought it very bitterly. They contended that the Democrats should have at least two of the six Congressmen and that an apportionment could have been made and should have been made with that end in view. The truth was that several of those who made such a stubborn fight against the bill had Congressional aspirations themselves and, of course, they did not fail to see that as drawn the bill did not hold out flattering hopes for the gratification of that ambition.   But it was all that Mr. Goar and a few others that he had taken into his confidence expected, or had any right to expect. In fact, the one Democratic district, constructed in accordance with their wishes, was just about what they wanted.   While they voted against the bill,— merely to be in accord with their party associates, — they insisted that there should be no filibustering or other dilatory methods adopted to defeat it. After a hard and stubborn fight, and after several days of exciting debate, the bill was finally passed by a strict party vote.   A few days later it passed the Senate without amendment, was signed by the Governor, and became a law.

As had been predicted by Mr. Goar, Hon. L. Q. C. Lamar was nominated by the Democrats for Congress in the first district, which was the Democratic district.   The Republicans nominated against him a very strong and able man, the Hon. R. W. Flournoy, who had served with Mr. Lamar as a member of the Secession Convention of 1861. He made an aggressive and brilliant canvass of the district, but the election of Mr. Lamar was a foregone conclusion, since the Democratic majority in the district was very large.

CHAPTER VI

FUSION OF DEMOCRATS AND REPUBLICANS IN THE STATE ELECTION OF 1873. REPUBLICAN VICTORY

An important election was to be held in Mississippi in 1873, at which State, district, and county officers, as well as members of the Legislature, were to be elected. The tenure of office for the State and county officers was four years. 1873, therefore, was the year in which the successors of those that had held office since 1869 had to be elected.

The legislature to be elected that year would elect the successor of Senator Ames as United States Senator. Senator Ames was the candidate named to succeed himself. For some unaccountable reason there had been a falling out between Senator Alcorn and himself, for which reason Senator Alcorn decided to use his influence to prevent the reëlection of Senator Ames. This meant that there would be a bitter factional fight in the party, because both Senators were popular with the rank and file of the party.

The fact was soon developed, however, that the people favored the return of Senator Ames to the

Senate. This did not necessarily mean opposition or unfriendliness to Senator Alcorn. It simply meant that both were to be treated fairly and justly, and that each was to stand upon his own record and merits, regardless of their personal differences.

If Senator Alcorn had been in Senator Ames' place the probabilities are that the sentiment of the party would have been just as strongly in his favor as it was at that time in favor of Ames. But on this occasion Senator Alcorn made the mistake of making opposition to Senator Ames the test of loyalty to himself. In this he was not supported even by many of his warmest personal and political friends. In consequence of the bitter fight that was to be made by Senator Alcorn to prevent the return of Senator Ames to the Senate, many of Senator Ames' friends advised him to become a candidate for the office of Governor. In that way, it was believed, he could command the situation, and thus make sure his election to succeed himself as Senator; otherwise it might be doubtful.

But this involved two important points which had to be carefully considered. First, it involved the retirement of Governor Powers, who was a candidate to succeed himself. Second, the candidate for Lieutenant-Governor would have to be selected with great care, since if that program were carried out he would be, in point of fact, the Governor of the State for practically the whole term.

After going over the situation very carefully with his friends and supporters Senator Ames decided to become a candidate for Governor, public announcement of which decision was duly made. This announcement seemed to have increased the intensity of Senator Alcorn's opposition to Senator Ames, for the former did not hesitate to declare that in the event of Ames' nomination for Governor by the regular party convention he would bolt the action of the convention, and make the race for Governor as an independent candidate. This declaration, however, made no impression upon the friends and supporters of Ames, and evidently had very little effect upon the rank and file of the party; for the fact became apparent shortly after the announcement of the candidacy of Ames that his nomination was a foregone conclusion. In fact, Senator Ames had such a strong hold upon the rank and file of the party throughout the State that when the convention met there was practically no opposition to his nomination. The friends and supporters of Governor Powers realized early in the campaign the hopelessness of the situation, so far as he was concerned, and therefore made no serious effort in his behalf.

What gave the Ames managers more concern than anything else was the selection of a suitable man for Lieutenant-Governor. Many of the colored delegates insisted that three of the seven men to be nominated should be of that race. The offices they insisted on filling were those of Lieutenant-Governor, Secretary of State, and Superintendent of Education. Since the colored men had been particularly loyal and faithful to Senator Ames it was not deemed wise to ignore their demands. But the question was, Where is there a colored man possessing the qualifications necessary to one in charge of the executive department of the state?

After going over the field very carefully it was decided that there was just one man possessing the necessary qualifications,—B. K. Bruce, of Bolivar County. He, it was decided, was just the man for the place, and to him the nomination was to be tendered. A committee was appointed to wait on Mr. Bruce and inform him of the action of the conference, and urge him to consent to the use of his name. But Mr. Bruce positively declined. He could not be induced under any circumstances to change his mind. He was fixed in his determination not to allow his name to be used for the office of Lieutenant-Governor, and from that determination he could not be moved.

Mr. Bruce's unexpected attitude necessitated a radical change in the entire program. It had been agreed that the Lieutenant-Governorship should go to a colored man, but after Bruce's declination the Ames managers were obliged to take one of

two men,— H. C. Carter, or A. K. Davis. Davis
was the more acceptable of the two; but neither,
it was thought, was a fit and suitable man to be
placed at the head of the executive department of
the State. After again going over the field, and
after canvassing the situation very carefully, it was
decided that Ames would not be a candidate to succeed himself as United States Senator, but that he
would be a candidate to succeed Senator Alcorn.
This decision, in all probability, would not have
been made if Alcorn had been willing to abide by
the decision of the convention. But, since he announced his determination to bolt the nomination
of his party for Governor and run as an Independent candidate, it was decided that he had forfeited any claim he otherwise would have had upon
the party to succeed himself in the Senate. Senator Alcorn's term would expire March 4, 1877.
His successor would be elected by the Legislature
that would be chosen in November, 1875. If Ames
should be elected to the Governorship his successor
in that office would be elected in November, 1877.
In the event of his election to the Senate to succeed
Senator Alcorn, his term as Senator would commence March 4, 1877, yet he could remain in the
office of Governor until the meeting of Congress
the following December, thus practically serving
out the full term as Governor.

With that plan mapped out and agreed upon,

and the party leaders committed to its support, Davis was allowed to be nominated for the office of Lieutenant-Governor. Two other colored men were also placed upon the State ticket,— James Hill, for Secretary of State, and T. W. Cardozo, for State Superintendent of Education. While Davis had made quite a creditable record as a member of the Legislature, it could not be said that his name added strength to the ticket. Hill, on the other hand, was young, active, and aggressive, and considerably above the average colored man in point of intelligence at that time. His nomination was favorably received, because it was generally believed that, if elected, he would discharge the duties of the office in a way that would reflect credit upon himself and give satisfaction to the public. In point of education and experience Cardozo was admitted to be entirely capable of filling the office of Superintendent of Education; but he was not well known outside of his own county, Warren. In fact his nomination was largely a concession to that strong Republican county.

The three white men nominated,— besides the candidate for Governor,— were, W. H. Gibbs, for Auditor of Public Accounts; Geo. E. Harris, for Attorney-General, and Geo. H. Holland, for State Treasurer. Gibbs had been a member of the Constitutional Convention of 1868, and subsequently a member of the State Senate. Holland had

served as a member of the Legislature from Oktib-
beha County.   Harris had been a member of Congress from the Second (Holly Springs) District,
having been defeated for the nomination in 1872 by
A. R. Howe, of Panola County.   While the ticket,
as a whole, was not a weak one, its principal strength
was in its head,— the candidate for Governor.

Shortly after the adjournment of the convention Senator Alcorn had another convention
called which nominated a ticket, composed exclusively of Republicans, with himself at its head for
Governor.   The Democrats at their convention endorsed the Alcorn ticket.   While it would seem
that this action on the part of the Democrats ought
to have increased Alcorn's chances of success, it
appears to have been a contributory cause of his
defeat.   Thousands of Republicans who were in
sympathy with the movement, and who would have
otherwise voted the Alcorn ticket, refused to do so
for the reason that if it had been elected the Democrats could have claimed a victory for their party.
On the other hand, both tickets being composed
exclusively of Republicans, thousands of Democrats refused to vote for either, while some of them
voted the Ames ticket.   At any rate the election
resulted in the success of the Ames ticket by a
majority of more than twenty thousand.   The regular Republicans also had a large majority in both
branches of the Legislature.

HON. B. K. BRUCE

United States Senator, 1875-1881

CHAPTER VII

As soon as the result of the election was known, the candidacy of B. K. Bruce, for United States Senator to succeed Senator Ames, was announced. Ames' term as Governor was to commence the first Monday in January, 1874. His term as Senator would expire March 4, 1875. Upon assuming the duties of Governor he had been obliged to tender his resignation as Senator; thus it devolved upon the incoming legislature to elect a Senator to serve out the unexpired term, as well as for the full term of six years. Bruce's candidacy was for the full term.

The secret of Mr. Bruce's positive refusal to allow his name to be used for the Lieutenant-Governorship, which would have resulted in making him Governor, was now revealed. He had had the Senatorship in mind at the time, but, of course, no allusion was made to that fact. As between the Senatorship and the Governorship he chose the former, which proved to be a wise decision, in view of subsequent events. It was soon developed that

77

he was the choice of a large majority of the Republican members of the Legislature, white as well as colored. His nomination by the party caucus, therefore, was a foregone conclusion. Before the legislature met, it had been practically settled that Mr. Bruce should be sent to the Senate for the long term and Ex-Superintendant of Education, H. R. Pease, should be elected to serve out the unexpired term of Governor-elect Ames.

This slate was approved by the joint legislative caucus without a hitch and the candidates thus nominated were duly elected by the Legislature,— not only by the solid Republican vote of that body, but the additional vote of State Senator Hiram Cassidy, Jr., who had been elected as a Democrat.

Senator Alcorn's keen disappointment and chagrin at the outcome of his fight with Governor Ames was manifested when Senator Bruce made his appearance to be sworn in as a Senator. It was presumed that Senator Alcorn, in accordance with the uniform custom on such occasions, would escort his colleague to the desk of the President of the Senate to be sworn in. This Senator Alcorn refused to do. When Mr. Bruce's name was called Senator Alcorn did not move; he remained in his seat, apparently giving his attention to his private correspondence. Mr. Bruce, somewhat nervous and slightly excited, started to the President's desk unattended. Senator Roscoe Conkling, of New

York, who was sitting near by, immediately rose and extended his arm to Mr. Bruce and escorted him to the President's desk, standing by the new Senator's side until the oath had been administered, and then tendering him his hearty congratulations, in which all the other Republican Senators, except Senator Alcorn, subsequently joined.

This gracious act on the part of the New York Senator made for him a lifelong friend and admirer in the person of Senator Bruce. This friendship was so strong that Senator Bruce named his first and only son Roscoe Conkling, in honor of the able, distinguished, and gallant Senator from New York.

Senator Alcorn's action in this matter was the occasion of considerable unfavorable criticism and comment, some of his critics going so far as to intimate that his action was due to the fact that Mr. Bruce was a colored man. But, from my knowledge of the man and of the circumstances connected with the case, I am satisfied this was not true. His antipathy to Mr. Bruce grew out of the fact that Mr. Bruce had opposed him and had supported Ames in the fight for Governor in 1873. So far as I have been able to learn, I am the only one of the Senator's friends and admirers who opposed his course in that contest that he ever forgave. He, no doubt, felt that I was under less personal obligations to him than many others who pursued the same course that I did, since he had never rendered me any effective personal or political service, except when he brought the Independent members of the House in line for me in the contest for Speaker of that body in 1872; and even then his action was not so much a matter of personal friendship for me as it was in the interest of securing an endorsement of his own administration as Governor.

In Mr. Bruce's case he took an entirely different view of the matter. He believed that he had been the making of Mr. Bruce. Mr. Bruce had come to the State in 1869 and had taken an active part in the campaign of that year. When the Legislature was organized it was largely through the influence of Governor Alcorn that he was elected Sergeant-at-arms of the State Senate. When the Legislature adjourned Governor Alcorn sent Bruce to Bolivar county as County Assessor. Bruce discharged the duties of that office in such a creditable and satisfactory manner that he was elected in 1871 Sheriff and Tax Collector of that important and wealthy county, the most responsible and lucrative office in the gift of the people of the county. He was holding that office when elected to the United States Senate. Senator Alcorn felt, therefore, that in taking sides against him and in favor of Ames in 1873 Mr. Bruce was guilty of gross ingratitude. This accounted for his action in refusing to escort Mr. Bruce to the President's desk to be sworn in as Senator. In this belief, however, he did Mr. Bruce a grave injustice, for I know that gratitude was one of Mr. Bruce's principal characteristics.

If Senator Alcorn had been a candidate from the start for the Republican nomination for Governor, Mr. Bruce, I am sure, would have supported him even as against Senator Ames. But it was known that the Senator had no ambition to be Governor. His sole purpose was to defeat Senator Ames at any cost, and that, too, on account of matters that were purely personal and that had no connection with party or political affairs. Mr. Bruce, like very many other friends and admirers of the Senator, simply refused to follow him in open rebellion against his own party. I am satisfied, however, that Mr. Bruce's race identity did not influence the action of Senator Alcorn in the slightest degree. As further evidence of that fact, his position and action in the Pinchback case may be mentioned. He spoke and voted for the admission of Mr. Pinchback to a seat in the Senate when such a staunch Republican as Senator Edmunds, of Vermont, opposed and voted against admission. In spite of Senator Alcorn's political defeat and humiliation in his own State, he remained true and loyal to the National Republican party to the end of his Senatorial term, which terminated with the beginning of the Hayes Administration. Up to that time he had strong hopes of the future of the Republican party at the South.

CHAPTER VIII

The administrations of Governor Alcorn and of
Governor Ames, the two Republican Governors,
who were products of Reconstruction,— both having been elected chiefly by the votes of colored men,
— were among the best with which that State was
ever blessed, the generally accepted impression to
the contrary notwithstanding. In 1869 Alcorn was
elected to serve for a term of four years. Ames
was elected to serve the succeeding term. Alcorn
was one of the old citizens of the State, and was
therefore thoroughly identified with its business, industrial, and social interests. He had been one
of the large and wealthy landowners and slave-
owners, and therefore belonged to that small but
select and influential class known as Southern aristocrats.

Alcorn had taken an active and prominent part
in public matters since his early manhood. Before
the War of the Rebellion he had served several
terms as a member of the Legislature. He represented his county, Coahoma, in the Secession Con-

vention of 1861. He was bitterly opposed to Secession and fought it bravely; but when he found himself in a hopeless minority he gracefully acquiesced in the decision of the majority and signed the ordinance of Secession. He also joined the Confederate Army and took an active part in raising troops for the same. He was made brigadier-general, and had command of the Confederate forces in Mississippi for a good while. But, since the President of the Confederacy did not seem to be particularly partial to him, he was not allowed to see very much field service.

When the war was over he took an active part in the work of rehabilitation and Reconstruction. He strongly supported the Andrew Johnson plan of Reconstruction, and by the Legislature that was elected under that plan he was chosen one of the United States Senators, but was not admitted to the seat to which he had been elected. When the Johnson plan of Reconstruction was repudiated and rejected by the voters of the Northern States, and when what was known as the Congressional Plan of Reconstruction was endorsed and approved, Alcorn decided that further opposition to that plan was useless and unwise, and he publicly advised acceptance of it. His advice having been rejected by the Democrats, nothing remained for him to do but to join the Republican party, which he did in the early part of 1869.

Since he was known to be a strong, able and influential man,— one who possessed the respect and confidence of the white people of the State regardless of party differences,— he was tendered the Republican nomination for the Governorship at the election that was to be held the latter part of that year. He accepted the nomination and was duly elected. He discharged the duties of the office in an able, creditable and satisfactory manner. The only point upon which the administration was at all subject to unfavorable criticism was the high rate of taxation to which the people were subjected for the support of the State Government; but the reader will see that this could hardly have been avoided at that particular time. In his message to the Legislature in January, 1910, Governor E. F. Noel accurately stated the principle by which an administration is necessarily governed in raising revenue to carry on the government. This is the same principle that governed the Alcorn administration when it took charge of the State Government in 1870. In that message Governor Noel said: " The amount of assessment determines the tax burden of each individual, corporation, town, and county. The Legislature or local authorities settle the amount necessary to be provided for their respective treasuries. If all property be assessed at the same rate,— whether for the full value or for ten per cent. of the value of the property,—the payment of each owner would be unaffected; for the higher the assessment, the lower the levy; the lower the assessment, the higher the levy. Our State revenue is mainly derived from a six mill ad valorem tax."

When the Alcorn administration took charge of the State Government the War had just come to a close. Everything was in a prostrate condition. There had been great depreciation in the value of real and personal property. The credit of the State was not very good. The rate of interest for borrowed money was high. To materially increase the bonded debt of the State was not deemed wise, yet some had to be raised in that way. To raise the balance a higher rate of taxation had to be imposed since the assessed valuation of the taxable property was so low.

The figures showing the assessed valuation of taxable property in the State and the receipts and disbursements prior to 1875 are not available, but, taking the figures for that year, the reader can form a pretty accurate idea of what the situation must have been prior to that time. In 1875 the assessed valuation of real and personal property, subject to taxation in the State, was $119,313,834. The receipts from all sources that year amounted to $1,-801,129.12. The disbursements for the same year were, $1,430,192.83.

Now let us see what the situation was after the

Ames administration had been in power about two years,— or half of the term for which it had been elected. According to a very carefully prepared statement that was made and published by an expert accountant in the State Treasurer's office in the latter part of 1875 the ad valorem rate of taxes for general purposes had been reduced from seven to four mills, and yet the amount paid into the Treasury was not only enough to meet all demands upon the State, but to make a material reduction in the bonded debt. The following is taken from that statement:

"An examination of the report of the State Treasurer, of the first of January, 1874, at which time the administration of Governor Ames commenced, exhibits the fact that the indebtedness of the State at that date, exclusive of the amounts to the credit of the Chickasaw and common school funds, balance of current funds on hand, and warrants in the Treasury belonging to the State, was $1,765,554.33 The amount of the tax of the previous year remaining uncollected on January first, 1874, and afterward collected, $944,261.51, should be deducted from the above amount, which will show the actual indebtedness of the State at that date to be $821,292.82. A further examination of the report of the same officer, for January first, 1875, shows the indebtedness, after deducting amounts to the credit of the Chickasaw and com-

mon school funds, balance of current funds on
hand and warrants in the Treasury belonging to
the State, to be, $1,707,056.24. Then by deduct-
ing the amount of the tax of the previous year remaining uncollected January first, 1875, and afterwards collected, $998,628.11, the result shows the
actual indebtedness on January first, 1875, to be
$708,428.13. The forthcoming annual report of
the State Treasurer, for January first, 1876, will
show the indebtedness of the State, exclusive of the
amounts to the credit of the Chickasaw and common school funds, the balance of current funds on
hand, and warrants in the Treasury belonging to
the State, to be $980,138.33. Then, by proceeding
again as above, and deducting the amount of the
tax of the previous year, uncollected on January
first, 1876, and now being rapidly paid into the
Treasury, at a low estimate, $460,000.00, we have as
an actual indebtedness of the State on January first,
1876, $520,138.33. Thus it will be seen that the
actual indebtedness of the State is but little over a
half million dollars, and that during the two years
of Governor Ames' administration the State debt
has been reduced from $821,292.82, on January
first, 1874, to $520,138.33, on January first, 1876,
or a reduction of more than three hundred thousand dollars in two years — upwards of one third
of the State debt wiped out in that time. Not only
has the debt been reduced as above, but the rate of

taxation for general purposes has been reduced from seven mills in 1873 to four mills in 1875."

Notwithstanding the fact that the rate of taxation under the administration of Governor Ames had been reduced as shown above from seven mills in 1873 to four mills in 1875 the amount paid into the State Treasury was substantially the same as that paid in prior years. This was due to the great appreciation in the value of taxable property. Then again, a material reduction in the rate of taxation was made possible because the public institutions had all been rebuilt and repaired and a sufficient number of school buildings had been erected, thus doing away with the necessity for a special levy for such purposes. From this showing it would seem as if it were reasonable to assume that if such an administration as the one then in power could have been retained a few years longer there would not only have been a still further reduction in the rate of taxation, but the payable debt of the State would have been entirely wiped out. Instead of this we find the conditions to be about as follows:

First. Shortly after the first reform State Treasurer had been in charge of that office it was developed that he was a defaulter to the amount of $315,612.19.

Second. Notwithstanding the immense increase in the value of taxable property from year to year, it appears from the official records that the rate of ad valorem tax for general purposes has been increased from four to six mills.

Third.   There has been a very heavy increase in what is known as the specific or privilege taxes, — that is, a specific sum that business and professional persons must pay for the privilege of doing business or of practicing their professions in the State.

Fourth.   The amounts now collected and paid out for the support of the State Government are more than double what they were a few years ago, thus showing extravagance, if not recklessness, in the administration of the affairs of the State,— the natural result of a condition by which the existence of but one political party is tolerated.

Fifth.   Notwithstanding the immense increase in the value of taxable property, and in spite of the enormous sums paid into the State Treasury each year, there has been a material increase in the bonded debt of the State.   In fact it has been necessary at different times to borrow money with which to pay the current expenses of the State Government.

The following statistics for three years, 1907, 1908 and 1909, would seem to substantiate the above statement:

The value of the taxable property of the State in 1907 was $373,584.960. Receipts from all sources that year were $3,391,127.15. Disbursements for the same period were $3,730,343.29. Excess of disbursements over receipts, $339,216.14.

In 1908 the value of taxable property was $383,-823,739. Receipts from all sources that year were $3,338,398.98. Disbursements, same period, $3,351,119.46. Excess of disbursements over receipts, $12,720.48.

In 1909 the value of taxable property was $393,-297,173. Receipts from all sources were $3,-303,963.65. Disbursements, same period, $3,315,-201.48. Excess of disbursements over receipts, $11,237.83.

On the first day of January, 1907, what is called the payable debt of the State was reported to be $1,253,029.07. On the first day of January, 1876, it was $520,138.33. Increase, $732,890.74.

CHAPTER IX

WHAT CONSTITUTES " NEGRO DOMINATION "

It is claimed that in States, districts, and counties, in which the colored people are in the majority, the suppression of the colored vote is necessary to prevent " Negro Domination,"— to prevent the ascendency of the blacks over the whites in the administration of the State and local governments. This claim is based upon the assumption that if the black vote were not suppressed in all such States, districts, and counties, black men would be supported and elected to office because they were black, and white men would be opposed and defeated because they were white.

Taking Mississippi for purposes of illustration, it will be seen that there has never been the slightest ground for such an apprehension. No colored man in that State ever occupied a judicial position above that of Justice of the Peace and very few aspired to that position. Of seven State officers only one, that of Secretary of State, was filled by a colored man, until 1873, when colored men were elected to three of the seven offices,—Lieutenant-Governor, Secretary of State, and State Superin-

tendent of Education. Of the two United States
Senators and the seven members of the lower house
of Congress not more than one colored man occupied a seat in each house at the same time. Of
the thirty-five members of the State Senate, and
of the one hundred and fifteen members of the
House,— which composed the total membership of
the State Legislature prior to 1874,— there were
never more than about seven colored men in the
Senate and forty in the lower house. Of the ninety-
seven members that composed the Constitutional
Convention of 1868 but seventeen were colored
men. The composition of the lower house of the
State Legislature that was elected in 1871 was as
follows:

Total membership, one hundred and fifteen.
Republicans, sixty-six; Democrats, forty-nine. Colored members, thirty-eight. White members,
seventy-seven. White majority, thirty-nine.

Of the sixty-six Republicans thirty-eight were
colored and twenty-eight, white. There was a
slight increase in the colored membership as a result of the election of 1873, but the colored men
never at any time had control of the State Government nor of any branch or department thereof, nor
even that of any county or municipality. Out of
seventy-two counties in the State at that time, electing on an average twenty-eight officers to a county,
it is safe to assert that not over five out of one

hundred of such officers were colored men. The State, district, county, and municipal governments were not only in control of white men, but white men who were to the manor born, or who were known as old citizens of the State — those who had lived in the State many years before the War of the Rebellion.   There was, therefore, never a time when that class of white men known as Carpet-baggers had absolute control of the State Government, or that of any district, county or municipality, or any branch or department thereof.   There was never, therefore, any ground for the alleged apprehension of negro domination as a result of a free, fair, and honest election in any one of the Southern or Reconstructed States.

And this brings us to a consideration of the question, What is meant by "Negro Domination?" The answer that the average reader would give to that question would be that it means the actual, physical domination of the blacks over the whites. But, according to a high Democratic authority, that would be an incorrect answer.   The definition given by that authority I have every reason to believe is the correct one, the generally accepted one.   The authority referred to is the late Associate Justice of the Supreme Court of the State of Mississippi, H. H. Chalmers, who, in an article in the *North American Review* about March, 1881, explained and defined what is meant or understood by the term " Negro Domination."

According to Judge Chalmers' definition, in order to constitute " Negro Domination " it does not necessarily follow that negroes must be elected to office, but that in all elections in which white men may be divided, if the negro vote should be sufficiently decisive to be potential in determining the result, the white man or men that would be elected through the aid of negro votes would represent " Negro Domination." In other words, we would have " Negro Domination " whenever the will of a majority of the whites would be defeated through the votes of colored men. If this is the correct definition of that term,— and it is, no doubt, the generally accepted one,— then the friends and advocates of manhood suffrage will not deny that we have had in the past " Negro Domination," nationally as well as locally, and that we may have it in the future. *If*

If that is the correct definition then we are liable to have " Negro Domination " not only in States, districts, and counties where the blacks are in the majority, but in States, districts and counties where they are few in numbers. If that is the correct definition of " Negro Domination,"— to prevent which the negro vote should be suppressed,— then the suppression of that vote is not only necessary

in States, districts, and counties in which the blacks
are in the majority, but in every State, district, and
county in the Union; for it will not be denied that
the primary purpose of the ballot,— whether the
voters be white or colored, male or female,— is to
make each vote decisive and potential. If the vote
of a colored man, or the vote of a white man, determines the result of an election in which he par-
ticipates, then the very purpose for which he was
given the right and privilege will have been accomplished, whether the result, as we understand it, be
wise or unwise.

In this connection it cannot and will not be denied
that the colored vote has been decisive and potential
in very many important National as well as local
and State elections. For instance, in the Presidential election of 1868, General Grant, the Republican
candidate, lost the important and pivotal State of
New York, a loss which would have resulted in
his defeat if the Southern States that took part in
that election had all voted against him. That they
did not do so was due to the votes of the colored
men in those States. Therefore Grant's first administration represented " Negro Domination."

Again, in 1876, Hayes was declared elected President by a majority of one vote in the electoral college. This was made possible by the result of the
election in the States of Louisiana, South Carolina,
and Florida, about which there was much doubt

and considerable dispute, and over which there was a bitter controversy. But for the colored vote in those States there would have been no doubt, no dispute, no controversy. The defeat of Mr. Hayes and the election of Mr. Tilden would have been an undisputed and an uncontested fact. Therefore, the Hayes administration represented " Negro Domination."

Again, in 1880, General Garfield, the Republican candidate for President, carried the State of New York by a plurality of about 20,000, without which he could not have been elected. It will not be denied by those who are well informed that if the colored men that voted for him in that State at that time had voted against him, he would have lost the State and, with it, the Presidency. Therefore, the Garfield-Arthur administration represented " Negro Domination."

Again, in 1884, Mr. Cleveland, the Democratic candidate, carried the doubtful but very important State of New York by the narrow margin of 1,147 plurality, which resulted in his election. It cannot and will not be denied that even at that early date the number of colored men that voted for Mr. Cleveland was far in excess of the plurality by which he carried the State. Mr. Cleveland's first administration, therefore, represented " Negro Domination." Mr. Cleveland did not hesitate to admit and appreciate the fact that colored men contributed largely to his success, hence he did not fail to give that element of his party appropriate and satisfactory official recognition.

Again, in 1888, General Harrison, the Republican Presidential candidate, carried the State of New York by a plurality of about 20,000, which resulted in his election, which he would have lost but for the votes of the colored men in that State. Therefore, Harrison's administration represented "Negro Domination."

The same is true of important elections in a number of States, districts and counties in which the colored vote proved to be potential and decisive. But enough has been written to show the absurdity of the claim that the suppression of the colored vote is necessary to prevent "Negro Domination." So far as the State of Mississippi is concerned, in spite of the favorable conditions, as shown above, the legitimate State Government,— the one that represented the honestly expressed will of a majority of the voters of the State,— was in the fall of 1875 overthrown through the medium of a sanguinary revolution. The State Government was virtually seized and taken possession of *vi et armis*. Why was this? What was the excuse for it? What was the motive, the incentive that caused it? It was not in the interest of good, efficient, and capable government; for that we already had. It was not on account of dishonesty, maladministration, misappropriation of public funds; for every dollar of the public funds had been faithfully accounted for. It was not on account of high taxes; for it had been shown that, while the tax rate was quite high during the Alcorn administration, it had been reduced under the Ames administration to a point considerably less than it is now or than it has been for a number of years. It was not to prevent " Negro Domination " and to make sure the ascendency of the whites in the administration of the State and local governments; for that was then the recognized and established order of things, from which there was no apprehension of departure. Then, what was the cause of this sudden and unexpected uprising? There must have been a strong, if not a justifiable, reason for it. What was it? That question will be answered in a subsequent chapter.

CHAPTER X

In the last preceding chapter it was stated that
the reason for the sanguinary revolution, which
resulted in the overthrow of the Republican state
government in the State of Mississippi in 1875,
would be given in a subsequent chapter. What was
true of Mississippi at that time was largely true
of the other Reconstructed States where similar results subsequently followed. When the War of the
Rebellion came to an end it was believed by some,
and apprehended by others, that serious and radical
changes in the previous order of things would necessarily follow.

But when what was known as the Johnson Plan
of Reconstruction was disclosed it was soon made
plain that if that plan should be accepted by the
country no material change would follow, for the
reason, chiefly, that the abolition of slavery would
have been abolition only in name. While physical
slavery would have been abolished, yet a sort of
feudal or peonage system would have been established in its place, the effect of which would have

been practically the same as the system which had been abolished. The former slaves would have been held in a state of servitude through the medium of labor-contracts which they would have been obliged to sign,— or to have signed for them, — from which they, and their children, and, perhaps, their children's children could never have been released. This would have left the old order of things practically unchanged. The large landowners would still be the masters of the situation, the power being still possessed by them to perpetuate their own potential influence and to maintain their own political supremacy.

But it was the rejection of the Johnson Plan of Reconstruction that upset these plans and destroyed these calculations. The Johnson plan was not only rejected, but what was known as the Congressional Plan of Reconstruction,— by which suffrage was conferred upon the colored men in all the States that were to be reconstructed,— was accepted by the people of the North as the permanent policy of the government, and was thus made the basis of Reconstruction and readmission of those States into the Union.

Of course this meant a change in the established order of things that was both serious and radical. It meant the destruction of the power and influence of the Southern aristocracy. It meant not only the physical emancipation of the blacks but the politi-

cal emancipation of the poor whites, as well. It
meant the destruction in a large measure of the
social, political, and industrial distinctions that had
been maintained among the whites under the old
order of things. But was this to be the settled
policy of the government? Was it a fact that the
incorporation of the blacks into the body politic of
the country was to be the settled policy of the government; or was it an experiment,— a temporary
expedient?

These were doubtful and debatable questions,
pending the settlement of which matters could not
be expected to take a definite shape. With the incorporation of the blacks into the body politic of the
country,— which would have the effect of destroy-
ing the ability of the aristocracy to maintain their
political supremacy, and which would also have the
effect of bringing about the political emancipation
of the whites of the middle and lower classes,—
a desperate struggle for political supremacy between the antagonistic elements of the whites was
inevitable and unavoidable. But the uncertainty
growing out of the possibility of the rejection by
the country of the Congressional Plan of Reconstruction was what held matters in temporary abeyance. President Johnson was confident,— or pre-
tended to be,— that as soon as the people of the
North had an opportunity to pass judgment upon
the issues involved, the result would be the ac-

ceptance of his plan and the rejection of the one proposed by Congress.

While the Republicans were successful in 1868 in not only electing the President and Vice-President and a safe majority in both branches of Congress, yet the closeness of the result had the effect of preventing the abandonment of the hope on the part of the supporters of the Johnson administration that the administration Plan of Reconstruction would ultimately be adopted and accepted as the basis of Reconstruction. Hence bitter and continued opposition to the Congressional Plan of Reconstruction was declared by the ruling class of the South to be the policy of that section. While the Republicans were again successful in the Congressional elections of 1870 yet the advocates of the Johnson plan did not abandon hope of the ultimate success and acceptance by the country of that plan until after the Presidential and Congressional elections of 1872. In the meantime a serious split had taken place in the Republican party which resulted in the nomination of two sets of candidates for President and Vice-President. The Independent or Liberal Republicans nominated Horace Greeley of New York, for President, and B. Gratz Brown, of Missouri, for Vice-President. The regular Republicans renominated President Grant to succeed himself, and for Vice-President, Senator Henry Wilson, of Massachusetts, was selected.

The Democratic National Convention endorsed the ticket that had been nominated by the Liberal Republicans. The Republicans carried the election by an immense majority. With two or three exceptions the electoral vote of every state in the Union was carried for Grant and Wilson. The Republicans also had a very large majority in both branches of Congress.

Since the result of the election was so decisive, and since every branch of the government was then in the hands of the Republicans, further opposition to the Congressional Plan of Reconstruction was for the first time completely abandoned. The fact was then recognized that this was the settled and accepted policy of the Government and that further opposition to it was useless. A few of the southern whites, General Alcorn being one of the number, had accepted the result of the Presidential and Congressional elections of 1868 as conclusive as to the policy of the country with reference to Reconstruction; but those who thought and acted along those lines at that time were exceptions to the general rule. But after the Presidential and Congressional elections of 1872 all doubt upon that subject was entirely removed.

The Southern whites were now confronted with a problem that was both grave and momentous. But the gravity of the situation was chiefly based upon the possibility,— if not upon a probability,—

of a reversal of what had been the established order of things, especially those of a political nature.

The inevitable conflict between the antagonistic elements of which Southern society was composed could no longer be postponed. But the colored vote was the important factor which now had to be considered and taken into account. It was conceded that whatever element or faction could secure the favor and win the support of the colored vote would be the dominant and controlling one in the State. It is true that between 1868 and 1872, when the great majority of Southern whites maintained a policy of "masterly inactivity," the colored voters were obliged to ultilize such material among the whites as was available; but it is a well-known fact that much of the material thus utilized was from necessity and not from choice, and that whenever and wherever an acceptable and reputable white man would place himself in a position where his services could be utilized he was gladly taken up and loyally supported by the colored voters.

After 1872 the necessity for supporting undesirable material no longer existed; and colored voters had the opportunity not only of supporting Southern whites for all the important positions in the State, but also of selecting the best and most desirable among them. Whether the poor whites or the aristocrats of former days were to be placed in control of the affairs of the State was a question

which the colored voters alone could settle and determine. That the colored man's preference should
be the aristocrat of the past was perfectly natural,
since the relations between them had been friendly,
cordial and amicable even during the days of slavery. Between the blacks and the poor whites the
feeling had been just the other way; which was
due not so much to race antipathy as to jealousy
and envy on the part of the poor whites, growing
out of the cordial and friendly relations between
the aristocrats and their slaves; and because the
slaves were, in a large measure, their competitors
in the industrial market. When the partiality of
the colored man for the former aristocrats became
generally known, they — the former aristocrats,—
began to come into the Republican party in large
numbers. In Mississippi they were led by such
men as Alcorn, in Georgia by Longstreet, in Virginia by Moseby, and also had as leaders such ex-
governors as Orr, of South Carolina; Brown, of
Georgia, and Parsons, of Alabama.

Between 1872 and 1875 the accessions to the
Republican ranks were so large that it is safe to
assert that from twenty-five to thirty per cent of
the white men of the Southern States were identified with the Republican party; and those who thus
acted were among the best and most substantial men
of that section. Among that number in the State
of Mississippi was J. L. Alcorn, J. A. Orr, J. B.

Deason, R. W. Flournoy, and Orlando Davis. In addition to these there were thousands of others, many of them among the most prominent men of the State. Among the number was Judge Hiram Cassidy, who was the candidate of the Democratic party for Congress from the Sixth District in 1872, running against the writer of these lines. He was one of the most brilliant and successful members of the bar in southern Mississippi. Captain Thomas W. Hunt, of Jefferson County, was a member of one of the oldest, best, and most influential families of the South. The family connections were not, however, confined to the South; George Hunt Pendelton of Ohio, for instance, who was the Democratic candidate for Vice-President of the United States on the ticket with McClellan, in 1864, and who was later one of the United States Senators from Ohio, was a member of the same family.

While the colored men held the key to the situation, the white men knew that the colored men had no desire to rule or dominate even the Republican party. All the colored men wanted and demanded was a voice in the government under which they lived, and to the support of which they contributed, and to have a small, but fair, and reasonable proportion of the positions that were at the disposal of the voters of the State and of the administration.

While the colored men did not look with favor

upon a political alliance with the poor whites, it must be admitted that, with very few exceptions, that class of whites did not seek, and did not seem to desire such an alliance. For this there were several well-defined reasons.

In the first place, while the primary object of importing slaves into that section was to secure labor for the cultivation of cotton, the slave was soon found to be an apt pupil in other lines of industry. In addition to having his immense cotton plantations cultivated by slave labor, the slave-owner soon learned that he could utilize these slaves as carpenters, painters, plasterers, bricklayers, blacksmiths and in all other fields of industrial occupations and usefulness. Thus the whites who depended upon their labor for a living along those lines had their field of opportunity very much curtailed. Although the slaves were not responsible for this condition, the fact that they were there and were thus utilized, created a feeling of bitterness and antipathy on the part of the laboring whites which could not be easily wiped out.

In the second place, the whites of that class were not at that time as ambitious, politically, as were the aristocrats. They had been held in political subjection so long that it required some time for them to realize that there had been a change. At that time they, with a few exceptions, were less efficient, less capable, and knew less about matters of state and governmental administration than many of the ex-slaves. It was a rare thing, therefore, to find one of that class at that time that had any political ambition or manifested any desire for political distinction or official recognition. As a rule, therefore, the whites that came into the leadership of the Republican party between 1872 and 1875 were representatives of the most substantial families of the land.

CHAPTER XI

After the Presidential election of 1872 no one could be found who questioned the wisdom or practicability of the Congressional Plan of Reconstruction, or who looked for its overthrow, change or modification. After that election the situation was accepted by everyone in perfect good faith. No one could be found in any party or either race who was bold enough to express the opinion that the Congressional Plan of Reconstruction was a mistake, or that negro suffrage was a failure. To the contrary it was admitted by all that the wisdom of both had been fully tested and clearly vindicated. It will not be denied even now by those who will take the time to make a careful examination of the situation, that no other plan could have been devised or adopted that could have saved to the country the fruits of the victory that had been won on the field of battle. The adoption of any other plan would have resulted in the accomplishment of nothing but the mere physical abolition of slavery and a denial of the right of a State to withdraw from the Union. These would have been mere abstract propositions, with no authority vested in the National Government for their enforcement.   The war for the Union would have been practically a failure.   The South would have gained and secured substantially everything for which it contended except the establishment of an independent government.   The black man, therefore, was the savior of his country, not only on the field of battle, but after the smoke of battle had cleared away.

Notwithstanding the general acceptance of this plan after the Presidential election of 1872, we find that in the fall of 1874 there was a complete and radical change in the situation,— a change both sudden and unexpected.   It came, as it were, in the twinkling of an eye.   It was like a clap of thunder from a clear sky.   It was the State and Congressional elections of that year.

In the elections of 1872 nearly every State in the Union went Republican.   In the State and Congressional elections of 1874 the result was the reverse of what it was two years before,— nearly every State going Democratic.   Democrats were surprised, Republicans were dumbfounded.   Such a result had not been anticipated by anyone.   Even the State of Massachusetts, the birthplace of abolitionism, the cradle of American liberty, elected a Democratic Governor.   The Democrats had a majority in the National House of Representatives that was about equal to that which the Republicans had elected two years before. Such veteran Republican leaders in the United States Senate as Chandler, of Michigan, Windom, of Minnesota, and Carpenter, of Wisconsin, were retired from the Senate. When the returns were all in it was developed that the Democrats did not have a clear majority on joint ballot in the Michigan Legislature, but the margin between the two parties was so close that a few men who had been elected as independent Republicans had the balance of power. These Independents were opposed to the reëlection of Senator Chandler. That the Democrats should be anxious for the retirement of such an able, active, aggressive, and influential Republican leader as Chandler was to be expected. That party, therefore, joined with the Independents in the vote for Senator which resulted in the election of a harmless old gentleman by the name of Christiancy. The Michigan situation was found to exist also in Minnesota, and the result was the retirement of that strong and able leader, Senator William Windom, and the election of a new and unknown man, McMillan.

What was true of Michigan and Minnesota was also found to be true of Wisconsin. The same sort of combination was made, which resulted in the retirement of the able and brilliant Matt Carpenter, and the election of a new man, Cameron, who was not then known outside of the boundaries of his State.   Cameron proved to be an able man, a useful Senator, a good Republican and an improvement, in some respects, upon his predecessor; but his election was a defeat of the Republican organization in his State, which, of course, was the objective point with the Democrats.

It was the State and Congressional elections of 1874 that proved to be the death of the Republican party at the South.   The party in that section might have survived even such a crushing blow as this, but for subsequent unfortunate events to which allusion has been made in a previous chapter, and which will be touched upon in some that are to follow.   But, under these conditions, its survival was impossible.   If the State and Congressional elections of 1874 had been a repetition of those of 1872 or if they had resulted in a Republican victory, Republican success in the Presidential election of 1876 would have been a reasonably assured fact.   By that time the party at the South would have included in its membership from forty to fifty per cent of the white men of their respective States and as a result thereof it would have been strong enough to stand on its own feet and maintain its own independent existence, regardless of reverses which the parent organization might have sustained in other sections. But at that time the party in that section was in

its infancy. It was young, weak, and comparatively helpless. It still needed the fostering care
and the protecting hand of the paternal source of
its existence.

When the smoke of the political battle that was
fought in the early part of November, 1874, had
cleared away, it was found that this strong, vigor-
ous and healthy parent had been carried from the
battle-field seriously wounded and unable to admin-
ister to the wants of its Southern offspring. The
offspring was not strong enough to stand alone.
The result was that its demise soon followed because it had been deprived of that nourishment,
that sustenance and that support which were essential to its existence and which could come only
from the parent which had been seriously if not
fatally wounded upon the field of battle. After
the Presidential election of 1872 Southern white
men were not only coming into the Republican
party in large numbers, but the liberal and pro-
gressive element of the Democracy was in the ascendency in that organization. That element,
therefore, shaped the policy and declared the principles for which that organization stood. This
meant the acceptance by all political parties of what
was regarded as the settled policy of the National
Government. In proof of this assertion a quota-
tion from a political editorial which appeared about
that time in the Jackson, Mississippi, *Clarion,*

— the organ of the Democratic party,— will not be out of place. In speaking of the colored people and their attitude towards the whites, that able and influential paper said:

" While they [the colored people] have been naturally tenacious of their newly-acquired privileges, their general conduct will bear them witness that they have shown consideration for the feelings of the whites. The race line in politics would never have been drawn if opposition had not been made to their enjoyment of equal privileges in the government and under the laws after they were emancipated."

In other words, the colored people had manifested no disposition to rule or dominate the whites, and the only color line which had existed grew out of the unwise policy which had previously been pursued by the Democratc party in its efforts to prevent the enjoyment by the newly-emancipated race of the rights and privileges to which they were entitled under the Constitution and laws of the country. But after the State and Congressional elections of 1874 the situation was materially changed. The liberal and conservative element of the Democracy was relegated to the rear and the radical element came to the front and assumed charge.

Subsequent to 1872 and prior to 1875 race proscription and social ostracism had been completely abandoned.   A Southern white man could become a Republican without being socially ostracized.   Such a man was no longer looked upon as a traitor to his people, or false to his race.   He no longer forfeited the respect, confidence, good-will, and favorable opinion of his friends and neighbors. Bulldozing, criminal assaults and lynchings were seldom heard of.   To the contrary, cordial, friendly and amicable relations between all classes, all parties, and both races prevailed everywhere. Fraud, violence, and intimidation at elections were neither suspected nor charged by anyone, for everyone knew that no occasion existed for such things. But after the State and Congressional elections of 1874 there was a complete change of front.   The new order of things was then set aside and the abandoned methods of a few years back were revived and readopted.

It is no doubt true that very few men at the North who voted the Republican ticket in 1872 and the Democratic ticket in 1874 were influenced in changing their votes by anything connected with Reconstruction.   There were other questions at issue, no doubt, that influenced their action.   There had been in 1873, for instance, a disastrous financial panic.   Then there were other things connected with the National Administration which met with popular disfavor.   These were the reasons, no doubt, that influenced thousands of Republicans to vote the Democratic ticket merely as an indication of their dissatisfaction with the National Administration.

But, let their motives and reasons be what they may, the effect was the same as if they had intended their votes to be accepted and construed as an endorsement of the platform declarations of the National Democratic Convention of 1868, at least so far as Reconstruction was concerned. Democrats claimed, and Republicans could not deny, that so far as the South was concerned this was the effect of the Congressional elections of 1874. Desertions from the Republican ranks at the South, in consequence thereof, became more rapid than had been the accessions between 1872 and 1875. Thousands who had not taken an open stand, but who were suspected of being inclined to the Republican party, denied that there had ever been any justifiable grounds for such suspicions. Many who had taken an open stand on that side returned to the fold of the Democracy in sackcloth and ashes,— upon bended knees, pleading for mercy, forgiveness and for charitable forbearance. They had seen a new light; and they were ready to confess that they had made a grave mistake, but, since their motives were good and their intentions were honest, they hoped that they would not be rashly treated nor harshly judged.

The prospects for the gratification and realization of the ambition of white men in that section had been completely reversed. The conviction became a settled fact that the Democratic party was the only channel through which it would be possible in the future for anyone to secure political distinction or receive official recognition,— hence the return to the ranks of that party of thousands of white men who had left it. All of them were eventually received, though some were kept on the anxious seat and held as probationers for a long time.

It soon developed that all that was left of the once promising and flourishing Republican party at the South was the true, faithful, loyal, and sincere colored men,— who remained Republican from necessity as well as from choice,— and a few white men, who were Republicans from principle and conviction, and who were willing to incur the odium, run the risks, take the chances, and pay the penalty that every white Republican who had the courage of his convictions must then pay. This was a sad and serious disappointment to the colored men who were just about to realize the hope and expectation of a permanent political combination and union between themselves and the better element of the whites, which would have resulted in good, honest, capable, and efficient local government and in the establishment and maintenance of peace, good-will, friendly, cordial, and amicable relations between the two races. But this hope, politically at least, had now been destroyed, and these expectations had been shattered and scattered to the four winds. The outlook for the colored man was dark and anything but encouraging. Many of the parting scenes that took place between the colored men and the whites who decided to return to the fold of the Democracy were both affecting and pathetic in the extreme.

The writer cannot resist the temptation to bring to the notice of the reader one of those scenes of which he had personal knowledge. Colonel James Lusk had been a prominent, conspicuous and influential representative of the Southern aristocracy of ante-bellum days. He enjoyed the respect and confidence of the community in which he lived,— especially of the colored people. He, like thousands of others of his class, had identified himself with the Republican party. There was in that community a Republican club of which Sam Henry, a well-known colored man, was president. When it was rumored,— and before it could be verified,— that Colonel Lusk had decided to cast his fortunes with the Republican party Henry appointed a committee of three to call on him and extend to him a cordial invitation to appear before the club at its next meeting and deliver an address. The invitation was accepted. As soon as the Colonel entered the door of the club, escorted by the committee, every man in the house immediately arose and all joined in giving three cheers and a hearty welcome to the gallant statesman and brave ex-Confederate soldier who had honored them with his distinguished presence on that occasion. He delivered a splendid speech, in which he informed his hearers that he had decided to cast his lot with the Republican party. It was the first public announcement of that fact that had been made. Of course he was honored, idolized and lionized by the colored people wherever he was known.

After the Congressional elections of 1874 Colonel Lusk decided that he would return to the ranks of the Democracy. Before making public announcement of that fact he decided to send for his faithful and loyal friend, Sam Henry, to come to see him at his residence, as he had something of importance to communicate to him. Promptly at the appointed time Henry made his appearance. He did not know for what he was wanted, but he had a well-founded suspicion, based upon the changed conditions which were apparent in every direction; hence, apprehension could be easily detected in his countenance. Colonel Lusk commenced by reminding Henry of the fact that it was before the club of which he was president and upon his invitation that he, Lusk, had made public announcement of his intention to act in the future with the Republican party. Now that he had decided to renounce any further allegiance to that party he thought that his faithful friend and loyal supporter, Sam Henry, should be the first to whom that announcement should be made. When he had finished Henry was visibly affected.

" Oh! no, Colonel," he cried, breaking down completely, " I beg of you do not leave us. You are our chief, if not sole dependence. You are our Moses. If you leave us, hundreds of others in our immediate neighborhood will be sure to follow your lead. We will thus be left without solid and substantial friends. I admit that with you party affiliation is optional. With me it is not. You can be either a Republican or a Democrat, and be honored and supported by the party to which you may belong. With me it is different. I must remain a Republican whether I want to or not. While it is impossible for me to be a Democrat it is not impossible for you to be a Republican. We need you. We need your prestige, your power, your influence, and your name. I pray you, therefore, not to leave us; for if you and those who will follow your lead leave us now we will be made to feel that we are without a country, without a home, without friends, and without a hope for the future. Oh, no, Colonel, I beg of you, I plead with you, don't go! Stay with us; lead and guide us, as you have so faithfully done during the last few years! "

Henry's remarks made a deep and profound impression upon Colonel Lusk. He informed Henry that no step he could take was more painful to him than this. He assured Henry that this act on his part was from necessity and not from choice.

"The statement you have made, Henry, that party affiliations with me is optional," he answered, "is presumed to be true; but, in point of fact, it is not. No white man can live in the South in the future and act with any other than the Democratic party unless he is willing and prepared to live a life of social isolation and remain in political oblivion. While I am somewhat advanced in years, I am not so old as to be devoid of political ambition. Besides I have two grown sons. There is, no doubt, a bright, brilliant and successful future before them if they are Democrats; otherwise, not. If I remain in the Republican party,— which can hereafter exist at the South only in name,— I will thereby retard, if not mar and possibly destroy, their future prospects. Then, you must remember that a man's first duty is to his family. My daughters are the pride of my home. I cannot afford to have them suffer the humiliating consequences of the social ostracism to which they may be subjected if I remain in the Republican party.

"The die is cast. I must yield to the inevitable and surrender my convictions upon the altar of my family's good,— the outgrowth of circumstances and conditions which I am powerless to prevent and cannot control. Henceforth I must act with the Democratic party or make myself a martyr; and I do not feel that there is enough at stake to justify me in making such a fearful sacrifice as that. It is, therefore, with deep sorrow and sincere regret, Henry, that I am constrained to leave you politically, but I find that I am confronted with a condition, not a theory. I am compelled to choose between you, on one side, and my family and personal interests, on the other. That I have decided to sacrifice you and yours upon the altar of my family's good is a decision for which you should neither blame nor censure me. If I could see my way clear to pursue a different course it would be done; but my decision is based upon careful and thoughtful consideration and it must stand."

Of course a stubborn and bitter fight for control of the Democratic organization was now on between the antagonistic and conflicting elements among the whites. It was to be a desperate struggle between the former aristocrats, on one side, and what was known as the "poor whites," on the other. While the aristocrats had always been the weaker in point of numbers, they had been the stronger in point of wealth, intelligence, ability, skill and experience. As a result of their wide experience, and able and skillful management, the aristocrats were successful in the preliminary struggles, as illustrated in the persons of Stephens, Gordon, Brown and Hill, of Georgia; Daniels and Lee, of Virginia; Hampton and Butler, of South Carolina; Lamar and Walthall, of Mississippi, and Garland, of Arkansas. But in the course of time and in the natural order of things the poor whites were bound to win. All that was needed was a few years' tutelage and a few daring and unscrupulous leaders to prey upon their ignorance and magnify their vanity in order to bring them to a realization of the fact that their former political masters were now completely at their mercy, and subject to their will.

That the poor whites of the ante-bellum period in most of the late slaveholding or reconstructed States are now the masters of the political situation in those States, is a fact that will not be questioned, disputed or denied by anyone who is well informed, or who is familiar with the facts. The aristocrats of ante-bellum days and their descendants in the old slave States are as completely under the political control and domination of the poor whites of the ante-bellum period as those whites were under them at that time. Yet the reader must not assume that the election returns from such States indicate the actual, or even the relative, strength of the opposing and antagonistic elements and factions. They simply indicate that the poor whites of the past and their descendants are now the masters and the leaders, and that the masters and the leaders of the past are now the submissive followers.

In the ranks of those who are now the recognized leaders is to be found some of the very best blood of the land,— the descendants of the finest, best, most cultivated, and most refined families of their respective States. But as a rule they are there, not from choice, but from necessity,— not because they are in harmony with what is being done, or because they approve of the methods that are being employed and pursued, but on account of circumstances and conditions which they can neither control nor prevent. They would not hesitate to raise the arm of revolt if they had any hope, or if they believed that ultimate success would be the result thereof. But as matters now stand they can detect no ray of hope, and can see no avenue of escape. Hence nothing remains for them to do but to hold the chain of political oppression and subjugation, while their former political subordinates rivet and fasten the same around their unwilling necks. They find they can do nothing but sacrifice their pride, their manhood, and their self-respect upon the altar of political necessity. They see, they feel, they fully realize the hopelessness of their condition and the helplessness of their situation. They see, they know, they acknowledge that in the line of political distinction and official recognition they can get nothing that their former political subordinates are not willing for them to have. With a hope of getting a few crumbs that may fall from the official table they make wry faces and pretend to be satisfied with what is being done, and with the way in which it is done. They are looked upon with suspicion and their loyalty to the new order of things is a constant source of speculation, conjecture, and doubt. But, for reasons of political expediency, a few crumbs are allowed occasionally to go to some one of that class, — crumbs that are gratefully acknowledged and thankfully received, upon the theory that some little consideration is better than none at all, especially in their present helpless and dependent condition. But even these small crumbs are confined to those who are most pronounced and outspoken in their declarations and protestations of loyalty, devotion, and subservient submission to the new order of things.

CHAPTER XII

The Mississippi Constitution having been ratified in 1869,— an odd year of the calendar,— caused the regular elections for State, district and county officers to occur on the odd year of the calendar, while the National elections occurred on the even years of the calendar, thus necessitating the holding of an election in the State every year. Therefore, no election was to be held in 1874, except for Congressmen, and to fill a few vacancies, while the regular election for county officers and members of the Legislature would be held in 1875.

Since the regular session of the 44th Congress would not convene before December, 1875, in order to avoid the trouble and expense incident to holding an election in 1874, the Legislature passed a bill postponing the election of members of Congress until November, 1875. There being some doubt about the legality of this legislation, Congress passed a bill legalizing the act of the Legislature. Consequently no election was held in the State in 1874 except to fill a few vacancies that had occurred in the Legislature and in some of the districts and counties.

One of the vacancies to be filled was that of State Senator, created by the resignation of Senator Hiram Cassidy, Jr. Senator Cassidy, who was elected as a Democrat in 1873, and who had voted for Mr. Bruce, the Republican caucus nominee, for United States Senator, had in the mean time publicly identified himself with the Republican party, thus following in the footsteps of his able and illustrious father, Judge Hiram Cassidy, Sr., who had given his active support to the Republican candidate for Governor in 1873.

Governor Ames had appointed Senator Cassidy a Judge of the Chancery Court, to accept which office it was necessary for him to resign his seat as a member of the State Senate. A special election was held in November, 1874, to fill that vacancy. The Democrats nominated a strong and able man, Judge R. H. Thompson, of Brookhaven, Lincoln County. The Republicans nominated a still stronger and abler man, Hon. J. F. Sessions, of the same town and county,— a Democrat who had represented Franklin County for several terms, but who had that year identified himself with the Republican party. Sessions was Chancellor Cassidy's law partner.

Since the counties comprising that senatorial district constituted a part of the district that I then represented in Congress, I took an active part in the support of the candidacy of Sessions. Although a Democrat, Hiram Cassidy, Jr., had been elected from that district in 1873, Sessions, a Republican, was elected by a handsome majority in 1874. A vacancy had also occurred in the Legislature from Franklin County, to fill which the Republicans nominated Hon. William P. Cassidy, brother of Chancellor Cassidy; but the Democratic majority in the county was too large for one' even so popular as Wm. P. Cassidy to overcome; hence he was defeated by a small majority.

From a Republican point of view Mississippi, as was true of the other reconstructed States, up to 1875 was all that could be expected and desired and, no doubt, would have remained so for many years, but for the unexpected results of the State and Congressional elections of 1874. While it is true, as stated and explained in a previous chapter, that Grant carried nearly every state in the Union at the Presidential election in 1872, the State and Congressional elections throughout the country two years later went just the other way, and by majorities just as decisive as those given the Republicans two years before.

Notwithstanding the severe and crushing defeat sustained by the Republicans at that time, it was claimed by some, believed by others, and predicted by many that by the time the election for President in 1876 would roll around it would be found that the Republicans had regained substantially all they had lost in 1874; but these hopes, predictions, and expectations were not realized. The Presidential election of 1876 turned out to be so close and doubtful that neither party could claim a substantial victory. While it is true that Hayes, the Republican candidate for President, was finally declared elected according to the forms of law, yet the terms and conditions upon which he was allowed to be peaceably inaugurated were such as to complete the extinction and annihilation of the Republican party at the South. The price that the Hayes managers stipulated to pay,— and did pay, — for the peaceable inauguration of Hayes was that the South was to be turned over to the Democrats and that the administration was not to enforce the Constitution and the laws of the land in that section against the expressed will of the Democrats thereof. In other words, so far as the South was concerned, the Constitution was not to follow the flag.

In the 43rd Congress which was elected in 1872 and which would expire by limitation March 4, 1875, the Republicans had a large majority in both Houses. In the House of Representatives of the 44th Congress, which was elected in 1874, the Democratic majority was about as large as was the Republican majority in the House of the 43rd Congress. The Republicans still retained control of the Senate, but by a greatly reduced majority.

During the short session of the 43rd Congress, important legislation was contemplated by the Republican leaders. Alabama was one of the States which the Democrats were charged with having carried in 1874 by resorting to methods which were believed to be questionable and illegal. An investigation was ordered by the House. A committee was appointed to make the investigation, of which General Albright, of Pennsylvania, was chairman. This committee was authorized to report by bill or otherwise. After a thorough investigation, the chairman was directed, and instructed by the vote of every Republican member of the committee, which constituted a majority thereof, to report and recommend the passage of what was called the Federal Elections Bill. This bill was carefully drawn; following substantially the same lines as a previous temporary measure, under the provisions of which what was known as the Ku Klux Klan had been crushed out, and order had been restored in North Carolina.

It is safe to say that this bill would have passed both Houses and become a law, but for the unexpected opposition of Speaker Blaine. Mr. Blaine was not only opposed to the bill, but his opposition was so intense that he felt it his duty to leave the Speaker's chair and come on the floor for the purpose of leading the opposition to its passage. This, of course, was fatal to the passage of the measure. After a desperate struggle of a few days, in which the Speaker was found to be in opposition to a large majority of his party associates, and which revealed the fact that the party was hopelessly divided, the leaders in the House abandoned the effort to bring the measure to a vote.

Mr. Blaine's motives in taking this unexpected position, in open opposition to the great majority of his party associates, has always been open to speculation and conjecture. His personal and political enemies charged that it was due to jealousy of President Grant. Mr. Blaine was a candidate for the Republican Presidential nomination the following year. It was a well-known fact that President Grant was not favorable to Mr. Blaine's nomination, but was in sympathy with the movement to have Senator Roscoe Conkling, of New York, Mr. Blaine's bitterest political enemy, nominated. Mr. Blaine was afraid, his enemies asserted, that, if the Federal Elections Bill,— under the provisions of which great additional power would have been conferred upon the President,— had become a law, that power would be used to defeat his nomination for the Presidency in 1876; hence his opposition to the Bill. But, whatever his motives were, his successful opposition to that measure no doubt resulted in his failure to realize the ambition of his life,—

the Presidency of the United States.   But for the stand he took on that occasion, he would probably have received sufficient support from Southern delegates in the National Convention to secure him the nomination, and, had he been nominated at that time, the probabilities are that he would have been elected.   But his opposition to that bill practically solidified the Southern delegates in that convention against him, and as a result he was defeated for the nomination, although he was the choice of a majority of the Northern delegates.

Even when Blaine received the nomination in 1884 it was developed that it could not have happened had the Southern delegates been as solidly against him at that time as they were in 1876.   But by 1884 the Southern Republicans had somewhat relented in their opposition to him, and, as a result thereof, he received sufficient support from that section to give him the nomination.   But he was defeated at the polls because the South was solid against him,— a condition which was made possible by his own action in defeating the Federal Elections Bill in 1875.   In consequence of his action in that matter he was severely criticised and censured by Republicans generally, and by Southern Republicans especially.

Although I was not favorable to his nomination for the Presidency at any time, my relations with Mr. Blaine had been so cordial that I felt at liberty to seek him and ask him, for my own satisfaction and information, an explanation of his action in opposing and defeating the Federal Elections Bill. I therefore went to him just before the final adjournment of the 43rd Congress and informed him that I desired to have a few minutes' private audience with him whenever it would be convenient for him to see me. He requested me to come to the Speaker's room immediately after the adjournment of the House that afternoon.

When I entered the room Mr. Blaine was alone. I took a seat only a few feet from him. I informed him of the great disappointment and intense dissatisfaction which his action had caused in defeating what was not only regarded as a party measure, but which was believed by the Republicans to be of vital importance from a party point of view, to say nothing of its equity and justice. I remarked that for him to array himself in opposition to the great majority of his own party associates,— and to throw the weight of his great influence against such an important party measure as the Federal Elections Bill was believed to be,— he must have had some motive, some justifiable grounds of which the public was ignorant, but about which I believed it was fair to himself and just to his own friends and party associates, that he give some explanation.

"As a southern Republican member of the House, and as one that is not hostile or particularly unfriendly to you," I said, " I feel that I have a right to make this request of you."

At first he gave me a look of surprise, and for several seconds he remained silent.   Then, straightening himself up in his chair, he answered:

" I am glad, Mr. Lynch, that you have made this request of me, since I am satisfied you are not actuated by any unfriendly motive in doing so.   I shall, therefore, give a frank answer to your question.   In my judgment, if that bill had become a law the defeat of the Republican party throughout the country would have been a foregone conclusion. We could not have saved the South even if the bill had passed, but its passage would have lost us the North; indeed, I could not have carried even my own State of Maine, if that bill had passed.   In my opinion, it was better to lose the South and save the North, than to try through such legislation to save the South, and thus lose both North and South. I believed that if we saved the North we could then look after the South.   If the Southern Democrats are foolish enough to bring about a Solid South the result will be a Solid North against a Solid South; and in that case the Republicans would have nothing to fear.   You now have my reasons, frankly and candidly given, for the action taken by me on the occasion referred to.   I hope you are satisfied with them."

I thanked Mr. Blaine cordially for giving me the

desired explanation. " I now feel better satisfied
with reference to your action upon that occasion,"
I assured him. " While I do not agree with you in
your conclusions, and while I believe your reason-
ing to be unsound and fallacious, still I cannot help
giving you credit for having been actuated by no
other motive than to do what you honestly believed
was for the best interest of the country and the
Republican party."

CHAPTER XIII

When I returned to my home after the adjournment of Congress in March, 1875, the political clouds were dark. The political outlook was discouraging. The prospect of Republican success was not at all bright. There had been a marked change in the situation from every point of view. Democrats were bold, outspoken, defiant, and determined. In addition to these unfavorable indications I noticed that I was not received by them with the same warmth and cordiality as on previous occasions. With a few notable exceptions they were cold, indifferent, even forbidding in their attitude and manner. This treatment was so radically different from that to which I had been accustomed that I could not help feeling it keenly. I knew it was indicative of a change in the political situation which meant that I had before me the fight of my life.

My advocacy and support of the Federal Elections Bill, commonly called the "Force Bill," was occasionally given as the reason for this change; but I knew this was not the true reason. In fact, that bill would hardly have been thought of but for the fact that Mr. Blaine, the Republican Speaker of the House, had attracted national attention to it through his action in vacating the chair and coming on the floor of the House to lead the opposition to its passage. This act on the part of the statesman from Maine made him, in the opinion of many Southern Democrats, the greatest man that our country had ever produced,— George Washington, the Father of the Republic, not excepted. They were loud in their thanks for the valuable service he had thus rendered them and, as evidence of their gratitude to him, they declared their determination to show their appreciation of this valuable service in a substantial manner whenever the opportunity presented itself for it to be done.

No man in the country was stronger, better or more popular than the statesman from Maine, until his name came before them as a candidate for President of the United States on a Republican ticket. A sudden transformation then took place. It was then discovered, to their great surprise and disappointment, that he was such an unsafe and dangerous man that no greater calamity could happen to the country than his elevation to the Presidency. Nothing, therefore, must be left undone to bring about his defeat.

I was well aware of the fact at the time that it was the result of the State and Congressional elections at the north in 1874 that had convinced Southern Democrats that Republican ascendency in the National Government would soon be a thing of the past — that the Democrats would be successful in the Presidential and Congressional elections of 1876 and that that party would, no doubt, remain in power for at least a quarter of a century. It was this, and not the unsuccessful effort to pass a Federal Elections Bill, that had produced the marked change that was noticeable on every hand. Every indication seemed to point to a confirmation of the impression that Democratic success at the Presidential election was practically an assured fact.

There had been a disastrous financial panic in 1873 which was no doubt largely responsible for the political upheaval in 1874; but that was lost sight of in accounting for that result. In fact they made no effort to explain it except in their own way. The Democrats had carried the country; the reasons for this they construed to suit themselves. The construction they placed upon it was that it was a national condemnation and repudiation of the Congressional Plan of Reconstruction, and they intended to govern themselves accordingly.

The election in Mississippi in 1875 was for members of Congress, members of the Legislature, and county officers, and also a State Treasurer to serve out the unexpired term of Treasurer Holland, deceased. My own renomination for Congress from

the Sixth (Natchez) District was a foregone conclusion, since I had no opposition in my own party;
but I realized the painful fact that a nomination
this time was not equivalent to an election.   Still,
I felt that it was my duty to make the fight, let the
result be what it might.

If Congressmen had been elected in 1874 the
State would have returned five Republicans and one
Democrat as was done in 1872; but in 1875 the prospect was not so bright, the indications were not so
favorable.   The Democrats nominated for State
Treasurer Hon. Wm. L. Hemmingway, of Carroll
County.   He was an able man, and had been quite
prominent as a party leader in his section of the
State.   The defiant attitude assumed, and the bold
declarations contained in the platform upon which
he was nominated were accepted by the Republicans as notice that the Democrats intended to carry
the election —" peaceably and fairly."

The Republicans nominated Hon. George M. Buchanan, of Marshall County, upon a platform which
strongly endorsed the National and State administrations.   Mr. Buchanan was a strong and popular
man.   He had been a brave and gallant Confederate soldier.   He had been for several years Sheriff
and Tax Collector of his county, and was known
to be especially fitted for the office of State Treasurer.   As Sheriff and Tax Collector of Marshall
County,— one of the wealthiest counties in the

State,— he had handled and disbursed many thousands of dollars, every dollar of which had been faithfully accounted for. His honesty, integrity, ability, fitness, and capacity, everyone, regardless of race or party, unhesitatingly admitted.

The administration of Governor Ames was one of the best the State had ever had. The judiciary was quite equal to that which had been appointed by Governor Alcorn. The public revenues had been promptly collected, and honestly accounted for. There had not only been no increase in the rate of taxation, but, to the contrary, there had been a material reduction. Notwithstanding these things the Democrats, together with the radical element in charge of the party machinery, determined to seize the State Government *vi et armis;* not because it was at all necessary for any special reason, but simply because conditions at that time seemed to indicate that it could be safely done.

After the nominations had all been made, the campaign was opened in dead earnest. Nearly all Democratic clubs in the State were converted into armed military companies. Funds with which to purchase arms were believed to have been contributed by the National Democratic organization. Nearly every Republican meeting was attended by one or more of those clubs or companies,— the members of which were distinguished by red shirts, indicative of blood,— the attendance being for the purpose, of course, of " keeping the peace and preserving order." To enable the Democrats to carry the State a Republican majority of between twenty and thirty thousand had to be overcome. This could be done only by the adoption and enforcement of questionable methods. It was a case in which the end justified the means, and the means had to be supplied.

The Republican vote consisted of about ninety-five per cent of the colored men, and of about twenty-five per cent of the white men. The other seventy-five per cent of the whites formerly constituted a part of the flower of the Confederate Army. They were not only tried and experienced soldiers, but they were fully armed and equipped for the work before them. Some of the colored Republicans had been Union soldiers, but they were neither organized nor armed. In such a contest, therefore, they and their white allies were entirely at the mercy of their political adversaries.

Governor Ames soon took in the situation. He saw that he could not depend upon the white members of the State militia to obey his orders, to support him in his efforts to uphold the majesty of the law, and to protect the law-abiding citizens in the enjoyment of life, liberty, and property. To use the colored members of the militia for such a purpose would be adding fuel to the flames. Nothing, therefore, remained for him to do but to call on the

National administration for military aid in his efforts to crush out domestic violence and enforce the laws of the State. He did call for such aid, but for reasons that will be given later it was not granted.

When the polls closed on the day of the election, the Democrats, of course, had carried the State by a large majority,— thus securing a heavy majority in both branches of the Legislature. Of the six members of Congress the writer was the only one of the regular Republican candidates that pulled through, and that, by a greatly reduced majority. In the Second (Holly Springs) District, G. Wiley Wells ran as an Independent Republican against A. R. Howe, the sitting member, and the regular Republican candidate for reëlection. The Democrats supported Wells, who was elected.

The delegation, therefore, consisted of four Democrats, one Republican, and one Independent Republican. While the delegation would have consisted of five straight Republicans and one Democrat had the election been held in 1874, still, since the Democrats had such a large majority in the House, the political complexion of the Mississippi delegation was not important. The election of the writer, it was afterwards developed, was due in all probability to a miscalculation on the part of some of the Democratic managers. Their purpose was to have a solid delegation, counting Wells as one of that number, since his election would be due to the support of the Democratic party.

But in my district the plan miscarried. In one of the counties there were two conflicting reports as to what the Democratic majority was; according to one, it was two hundred and fifty, according to the other, it was five hundred. The report giving two hundred and fifty was, no doubt, the correct one, but the other would probably have been accepted had it been believed at the time that it was necessary to insure the election of the Democratic candidate. To overcome the majority in that district was more difficult than to overcome it in any of the other districts. While their candidate, Colonel Roderick Seal, was quite a popular man, it was well known that I would poll a solid Republican vote and some Democratic votes in addition. Fortunately for me there was a split in the party in my own county (Adams) for county officers, which resulted in bringing out a very heavy vote. This split also made the count of the ballots very slow,— covering a period of several days. My name was on both tickets. The election took place on Tuesday, but the count was not finished until the following Friday evening. Hence, the result for member of Congress in that county could not be definitely ascertained until Friday night.

The Democratic managers at the State Capital were eager to know as soon as possible what the

Republican majority in Adams County would be for Congressman, hence, on Wednesday evening, the editor of the local Democratic paper received a telegram from the Secretary of the Democratic State Committee, requesting to be informed immediately what the Republican majority for Congressman would be in Adams County. The editor read the telegram to me and asked what, in my opinion, would be my majority in the county. My reply was that I did not think it would exceed twelve hundred; whereupon he sent in the following report: "Lynch's majority in Adams will not exceed twelve hundred."

Upon receipt of this telegram the majority of two hundred and fifty instead of five hundred was deemed sufficient from the county heretofore referred to. If the Republican majority in Adams would not exceed twelve hundred, the success of the Democratic Congressional candidate by a small but safe majority was assured on the face of the returns. Since Adams was the last county to be reported, no change could thereafter be made. When the count was finally finished in Adams it was found I had a majority of over eighteen hundred. This gave me a majority in the district of a little over two hundred on the face of the returns.

The disappointment and chagrin on the part of the Democratic managers can better be imagined than described. But the agreeable surprise to the

Republicans was at least equal to the Democrats' disappointment. The defeated Democratic candidate threatened to make a contest for the seat on the ground of violence and fraud; but this was so ridiculous that the managers of his own party would not allow him to carry the threat into execution.

CHAPTER XIV

Shortly after I reached Washington in the latter part of November, 1875, I called on the President to pay my respects, and to see him on business relating to a Civil Service order that he had recently issued, and that some of the Federal office-holders had evidently misunderstood. Postmaster Pursell, of Summit, an important town in my district, was one of that number. He was supposed to be a Republican, having been appointed as such. But he not only refused to take any part in the campaign of 1875, but he also declined to contribute a dollar to meet the legitimate expenses of that campaign. The President's Civil Service order was his excuse. According to Pursell's construction of that order, Federal office-holders must not only take no part in political or party campaigns, but they must make no contributions for political purposes. He not only said nothing and did nothing in the interest of his party in that campaign, but it was believed by some that he did not even vote the Republican ticket.

After paying my respects to the President I

brought this case to his attention. I informed him that I very much desired to have Postmaster Pursell removed, and a good Republican appointed in his stead.

"What is the matter with him?" the President asked. "Is he not a good postmaster?"

"Yes," I replied, "there is nothing to be said against him, so far as I know, with reference to his administration of the office. I only object to him on account of politics. He may be,— and no doubt is,— a good, capable, and efficient postmaster; but politically he is worthless. From a party point of view he is no good. In my opinion, there ought to be a man in that office who will not only discharge his duties in a creditable manner, but who will also be of some service to the party and to the administration under which he serves. In the present postmaster of the town of Summit we have not such a man, but we can and will have one if you will appoint the one whose name I now present and for whom I ask your favorable consideration. We had, as you know, a bitter and desperate struggle. It was the very time that we stood sadly in need of every man and of every vote. We lost the county that Summit is in by a small majority. If an active and aggressive man, such as the one whose name I now place before you, had been postmaster at Summit, the result in that County might have been different. I therefore earnestly recommend that Pursell be removed, and that Mr. Garland be appointed to succeed him."

The President replied: "You have given good and sufficient reasons for a change. Leave with me the name of the man you desire to have appointed, and his name will be sent to the Senate as soon as Congress meets." I cordially thanked the President, and assured him that he would have no occasion to regret making the change. In explanation of his Civil Service order the President remarked that quite a number of office-holders had seemed to misunderstand it, although it was plainly worded, and, as he thought, not difficult to understand. There had never been any serious complaints growing out of active participation in political campaigns on the part of office-holders, and that it was not, and never had been, the purpose of the administration, by executive order or otherwise, to limit or restrict any American citizen in the discharge of his duties as a citizen, simply because he happened to be an office-holder, provided that in so doing he did not neglect his official duties. There had, however, been serious complaints from many parts of the country about the use and abuse of Federal patronage in efforts to manipulate party conventions, and to dictate and control party nominations. To destroy this evil was the primary purpose of the civil service order referred to.

I told the President that his explanation of the

order was in harmony with my own construction and interpretation of it. That is why I made the recommendation for a change in the postmastership at Summit. The change was promptly made. I then informed the President that there was another matter about which I desired to have a short talk with him, that was the recent election in Mississippi. After calling his attention to the sanguinary struggle through which we had passed, and the great disadvantages under which we labored, I reminded him of the fact that the Governor, when he saw that he could not put down without the assistance of the National Administration what was practically an insurrection against the State Government, made application for assistance in the manner and form prescribed by the Constitution, with the confident belief that it would be forthcoming. But in this we were, for some reason, seriously disappointed and sadly surprised. The reason for this action, or rather non-action, was still an unexplained mystery to us. For my own satisfaction and information I should be pleased to have the President enlighten me on the subject.

The President said that he was glad I had asked him the question, and that he would take pleasure in giving me a frank reply. He said he had sent Governor Ames' requisition to the War Department with his approval and with instructions to have the necessary assistance furnished without delay. He had also given instructions to the Attorney-General to use the marshals and the machinery of the Federal judiciary as far as possible in coöperation with the War Department in an effort to maintain order and to bring about a condition which would insure a peaceable and fair election.   But before the orders were put into execution a committee of prominent Republicans from Ohio had called on him.   (Ohio was then an October State,— that is, her elections took place in October instead of November.)   An important election was then pending in that State. This committee, the President stated, protested against having the requisition of Governor Ames honored.   The committee, the President said, informed him in a most emphatic way that if the requisition of Governor Ames were honored, the Democrats would not only carry Mississippi,— a State which would be lost to the Republicans in any event,— but that Democratic success in Ohio would be an assured fact.   If the requisition were not honored it would make no change in the result in Mississippi, but that Ohio would be saved to the Republicans.   The President assured me that it was with great reluctance that he yielded,— against his own judgment and sense of official duty,— to the arguments of this committee, and directed the withdrawal of the orders which had been given the Secretary of War and the Attorney-General in that matter.

This statement, I confess, surprised me very much.

"Can it be possible," I asked, "that there is such a prevailing sentiment in any State in the North, East or West as renders it necessary for a Republican President to virtually give his sanction to what is equivalent to a suspension of the Constitution and laws of the land to insure Republican success in such a State? I cannot believe this to be true, the opinion of the Republican committee from Ohio to the contrary notwithstanding. What surprises me more, Mr. President, is that you yielded and granted this remarkable request. That is not like you. It is the first time I have ever known you to show the white feather. Instead of granting the request of that committee, you should have rebuked the men, — told them that it is your duty as chief magistrate of the country to enforce the Constitution and laws of the land, and to protect American citizens in the exercise and enjoyment of their rights, let the consequences be what they may; and that if by doing this Ohio should be lost to the Republicans it ought to be lost. In other words, no victory is worth having if it is to be brought about upon such conditions as those,— if it is to be purchased at such a fearful cost as was paid in this case."

"Yes," said the President, "I admit that you are right. I should not have yielded. I believed at the time that I was making a grave mistake. But as presented, it was duty on one side, and party obligation on the other. Between the two I hesitated, but finally yielded to what was believed to be party obligation. If a mistake was made, it was one of the head and not of the heart. That my heart was right and my intentions good, no one who knows me will question. If I had believed that any effort on my part would have saved Mississippi I would have made it, even if I had been convinced that it would have resulted in the loss of Ohio to the Republicans. But I was satisfied then, as I am now, that Mississippi could not have been saved to the party in any event and I wanted to avoid the responsibility of the loss of Ohio, in addition. This was the turning-point in the case.

"And while on this subject," the President went on, "let us look more closely into the significance of this situation. I am very much concerned about the future of our country. When the War came to an end it was thought that four things had been brought about and effectually accomplished as a result thereof. They were: first, that slavery had been forever abolished; second, that the indissolubility of the Federal Union had been permanently established and universally recognized; third, that the absolute and independent sovereignty of the several States was a thing of the past; fourth, that a national sovereignty had been at last created and established, resulting in sufficient power being vested in the general government not only to guarantee to every State in the Union a Republican form of government, but to protect, when necessary, the individual citizen of the United States in the exercise and enjoyment of the rights and privileges to which he is entitled under the Constitution and laws of his country. In other words, that there had been created a National citizenship as distinguished from State citizenship, resulting in a paramount allegiance to the United States,— the general Government,— having ample power to protect its own citizens against domestic and personal violence whenever the State in which he may live should fail, refuse, or neglect to do so. In other words, so far as citizens of the United States are concerned, the States in the future would only act as agents of the general Government in protecting the citizens of the United States in the enjoyment of life, liberty, and property. This has been my conception of the duties of the President, and until recently I have pursued that course. But there seems to be a number of leading and influential men in the Republican party who take a different view of these matters. These men have used and are still using their power and influence, not to strengthen but to cripple the President and thus prevent him from enforcing the Constitution and laws along these lines. They have not only used their power and influence to prevent and defeat wise and necessary legislation for these purposes, but they have contributed, through the medium of public meetings and newspaper and magazine articles, to the creation of a public sentiment hostile to the policy of the administration. Whatever their motives may be, future mischief of a very serious nature is bound to be the result. It requires no prophet to foresee that the national government will soon be at a great disadvantage and that the results of the war of the rebellion will have been in a large measure lost. In other words, that the first two of the four propositions above stated will represent all that will have been accomplished as a result of the war, and even they, for the lack of power of enforcement in the general government, will be largely of a negative character. What you have just passed through in the State of Mississippi is only the beginning of what is sure to follow. I do not wish to create unnecessary alarm, nor to be looked upon as a prophet of evil, but it is impossible for me to close my eyes in the face of things that are as plain to me as the noonday sun."

It is needless to say that I was deeply interested in the President's eloquent and prophetic talk which subsequent events have more than fully verified.

CHAPTER XV

The Presidential election was held in 1876. The Republicans had carried the country in 1872 by such a decisive majority that it indicated many years of continued Republican ascendency in the National Government. But the severe reverses sustained by that party at the polls two years later completely changed this situation and outlook. Democrats confidently expected and Republicans seriously apprehended that the Presidential election of 1876 would result in a substantial Democratic victory. Mr. Blaine was the leading candidate for the Republican nomination, but he had bitter opposition in the ranks of his own party. That opposition came chiefly from friends and supporters of Senator Conkling at the North and from Southern Republicans generally. The opposition of the Conkling men to Mr. Blaine was largely personal; while southern Republicans were opposed to him on account of his having caused the defeat of the Federal Elections Bill. The great majority of southern Republicans supported Senator Oliver P. Morton of Indiana.

After the National Convention had been organized, it looked for a while as if Mr. Blaine's nomination was a foregone conclusion. Hon. Edward McPherson, of Pennsylvania,— a strong Blaine man,— had been made President of the Convention. In placing Mr. Blaine's name in nomination, Hon. Robert G. Ingersoll of Illinois made such an eloquent and effective speech that he came very near carrying the Convention by storm, and thus securing the nomination of the statesman from Maine. But the opposition to Mr. Blaine was too well organized to allow the Convention to be stampeded, even by the power and eloquence of an Ingersoll. It was this speech that gave Mr. Ingersoll his national fame and brought him to the front as a public speaker and lecturer. It was the most eloquent and impressive speech that was delivered during the sitting of the Convention. After a bitter struggle of many hours, and after a number of fruitless ballots, the Convention finally nominated Gov. R. B. Hayes, of Ohio, as a compromise candidate. This result was brought about through a union of the combined opposition to Mr. Blaine. Hon. Wm. A. Wheeler, of New York, was nominated for Vice-President and the work of the Convention was over.

The Democrats nominated ex-Governor Samuel J. Tilden, of New York, for President, and Thomas

A. Hendricks, of Indiana, for Vice-President. Their platform pledged many radical reforms in the administration of the government. This ticket was made with the hope that it would be successful in the doubtful and debatable States of New York, New Jersey, Indiana, and Connecticut, which, with the Solid South, would constitute a majority of the electoral college, even if all the other States should go Republican, which was not anticipated.

That the prospect of Democratic success was exceedingly bright and the probability of a Republican victory extremely dark, was generally conceded. The South was counted upon to be solid in its support of the Democratic ticket, for the methods that had been successfully inaugurated in Mississippi the year before, to overcome a Republican majority of more than twenty thousand, were to be introduced and adopted in all the other States of that section in which conditions were practically the same as in Mississippi.

To insure success, therefore, it was only necessary for the Democrats to concentrate their efforts upon the four doubtful States outside of the Solid South. Up to a certain point the plan worked well. Every indication seemed to point to its successful consummation. As had been anticipated, the Democrats were successful in the four doubtful Northern States, and they also carried, on the face of the returns, every Southern State, just as had been planned; the Mississippi methods having been adopted in such of them as had Republican majorities to overcome. Since through those methods the Democrats had succeeded in overcoming a large Republican majority in Mississippi, there was no reason why the same methods should not produce like results in South Carolina, in Louisiana, and in Florida. In fact, it was looked upon as a reflection upon the bravery and party loyalty of the Democracy of those States if they could not do what had been done under like conditions in Mississippi. Hence those States *had* to be carried, "peaceably and fairly," of course, "but they must be carried just the same." Failure to carry them was out of the question, because too much was involved. According to the plans and calculations that had been carefully made, no Southern State could be lost. While it might be possible to win without all of them, still it was not believed to be safe to run any such risk, or take any such chance. If the Democrats should happen to carry a state that was not included in the combination, so much the better.

Everything seemed to work admirably. That it was a plan by which elections could be easily carried, with or without votes, had been clearly demonstrated. On the face of the returns the majorities were brought forth just as had been ordered and directed. But it seems that such methods had been anticipated by the Republican governments in South

Carolina, Louisiana, and Florida, and that suitable steps had been taken to prevent their successful consummation through the medium of State Returning Boards. When the Returning Boards had rejected and thrown out many of the majorities that had been returned from some of the counties and parishes, the result was changed, and the Republican candidates for Presidential electors were officially declared elected. This gave the Republican candidates for President and Vice-President a majority of one vote in the Electoral College. It has, of course, been alleged by many,— and it is believed by some,— that the actions of those Returning Boards defeated the will of the people as expressed at the polls, thus bringing about the seating in the Presidential chair of the man that had been fairly and honestly defeated. Yet, no one who is familiar with the facts, and who is honest enough to admit them, will deny that but for the inauguration in South Carolina, Florida, and Louisiana, of the Mississippi methods, those three States would have been as safely Republican at that time and in that election as were the States of Pennsylvania and Vermont. But the plans of the Democratic managers had been defeated. It was hard for them to lose a victory they felt and believed to have been won by them, notwithstanding the extraneous methods that had been employed to bring about such results.

CHAPTER XVI

EFFECTS OF THE REFORM ADMINISTRATION IN MISSISSIPPI

Because the Democrats carried the election in Mississippi in 1875, they did not thereby secure control of the State Government. That election was for members of the Legislature, members of Congress and county officers. Only one State officer was elected,— a State Treasurer,— to fill the vacancy created by the death of Treasurer Holland. All the other State officers were Republicans. But the Democrats could not afford to wait until Governor Ames' term expired. They were determined to get immediate control of the State Government. There was only one way in which this could be done, and that was by impeachment.

This course they decided to take. It could not be truthfully denied that Governor Ames was a clean, pure, and honest man. He had given the State an excellent administration. The State judiciary had been kept up to the high standard established by Governor Alcorn. Every dollar of the public money had been collected, and honestly accounted for. The State was in a prosperous condi-

tion. The rate of taxation had been greatly reduced, and there was every prospect of a still further
reduction before the end of his administration. But
these facts made no difference to those who were
flushed with the victory they had so easily won.
They wanted the offices, and were determined to
have them, and that, too, without very much delay.
Hence, impeachment proceedings were immediately
instituted against the Governor and Lieutenant-
Governor,— not in the interest of reform, of good
government or of low taxes, but simply in order to
get possession of the State Government.

The weakness of the case against the Governor
was shown when it developed that the strongest
charge against him was that he had entered into an
alleged corrupt bargain with State Senator Cassidy,
resulting in Cassidy's appointment as one of the
Judges of the Chancery Court. Cassidy had been
elected a member of the State Senate as a Democrat.
Notwithstanding that fact he voted for Mr. Bruce,
the Republican caucus nominee for United States
Senator, and subsequently publicly identified himself with the Republican party. Later his brother,
William P. Cassidy, and his law partner, Hon. J.
F. Sessions, did likewise. In 1874 Sessions was
elected to the State Senate as a Republican to serve
out the unexpired term of his law partner, Cassidy,
who had resigned his seat in the Senate upon his appointment as a Judge of the Chancery Court.

Cassidy was a brilliant young man, and an able lawyer. That the Governor should have selected him for an important judicial position was both wise and proper. It was one of his best and most creditable appointments and was generally commended as such when it was made. The fact that he had been elected to the State Senate as a Democrat, and shortly thereafter joined the Republican party was made the basis of the charge that his change of party affiliation was the result of a corrupt bargain between the Governor and himself, for which the Governor, but not the Judge, should be impeached and removed from office. There were a few other vague and unimportant charges, but this one, as weak as it was, was the strongest of the number.

When the articles of impeachment were presented to the House, it was seen that they were so weak and so groundless that the Governor believed it would be an easy matter for him to discredit them even before an antagonistic legislature. With that end in view, he employed several of the ablest lawyers in the country to represent him. Thy came to Jackson and commenced the preparation of the case, but it did not take them long to find out that their case was a hopeless one. They soon found out to their entire satisfaction that it was not to be a judicial trial, but a political one and that the jury was already prepared for conviction without regard to the law, the Constitution, the evidence, or the facts. Governor Ames was to be convicted, not because he was guilty of any offense, but because he was in the way of complete Democratic control of the State Government.

Personally they had nothing against Ames. It was not the man but the office they wanted, and that they were determined to have. They knew he had committed no offense, but, as matters then stood, being a Republican was an offense which justified removal from office. To punish him otherwise, for anything he had done or failed to do, did not at any time enter into their calculations. The Governorship was the prize at stake. In this matter there was no concealment of their purposes and intentions. As soon as the Governor's legal advisers found out what the actual situation was, they saw it was useless to continue the fight. Upon their advice, therefore, the Governor tendered his resignation, which was promptly accepted. He then left the State never to return again. If the impeachment proceedings had been instituted in good faith,— upon an honest belief that the chief executive had committed offenses which merited punishment,— the resignation would not have been accepted. The fact that it was accepted,— and that, too, without hesitation or question,— was equivalent to a confession that the purpose of the proceedings was to get possession of the office. Short work was made of the Lieutenant-Governor's case; and State Senator John M. Stone, the Democratic President pro tem. of the State Senate, was duly sworn in and installed as the acting Governor of the State.   Thus terminated a long series of questionable acts, the inauguration of which had no other purpose than to secure the ascendency of one political party over another in the administration of the government of the State.

The sanguinary revolution in the State of Mississippi in 1875 was claimed to be in the interest of good administration and honest government; it was an attempt to wrest the State from the control of dishonest men,— negroes, carpet baggers, and scalawags,— and place it in control of intelligent, pure, and honest white men.   With that end in view, Geo. M. Buchanan, a brave and gallant ex-Confederate soldier, was, through questionable and indefensible methods, defeated for the office of State Treasurer, and Wm. L. Hemmingway was declared elected. Yet when the change took place it was found that every dollar of the public money was accounted for.   During the whole period of Republican administration not a dollar had been misappropriated, nor had there been a single defalcation, although millions of dollars had passed through the hands of the fiscal agents of the State and of the different counties.

How was it with the new reform administration? Treasurer Hemmingway had been in office only a comparatively short while when the startling information was given out that he was a defaulter to the amount of $315,612.19. William L. Hemmingway a defaulter! Could such a thing be possible? Yes, it was an admitted and undisputed fact.

Mr. Hemmingway had been quite prominent in the politics of the State; but those who knew the man, and I was one of those, had every reason to believe that he was an honest man, and that he was the personification of integrity. He was neither a speculator nor a gambler. Even after the defalcation was made known there was nothing to indicate that any part of the money had been appropriated to his own use. Yet the money had mysteriously disappeared. Where was it? Who had it? These were questions the people of the State desired to have answered, but they have never yet been answered and, it is safe to say, they never will be. Hemmingway no doubt could and can answer those questions, but he has not done so and the probabilities are that he never will. He evidently believed that to turn State's evidence would render him more culpable than to be guilty of the act which he had allowed to be committed. He might have been forced to make a confession, or at least been compelled to give the prosecution a clue to the real criminal or criminals if the prosecution had been in charge of persons who could not be suspected of being the political beneficiaries of the methods by which it was possible for him to be placed in charge of the office. It was hardly reasonable to expect such men to make very much of an effort to secure a confession. In fact, it seems to have been a relief to them to have the accused take the position that he alone was the responsible party and that he was willing to bear all the blame and assume all the consequences that would result from the act. The names, therefore, of those who were the beneficiaries of this remarkable defalcation will, no doubt, remain a secret in the bosom of William L. Hemmingway, and will be buried with him in his grave.

Hemmingway was tried, convicted, sentenced and served a term in the State Prison; all of which he calmly endured rather than give the name of any person having connection with that unfortunate affair. All the satisfaction that the public can get with reference to it,—other than the punishment to which Hemmingway was subjected,—is to indulge in conjectures about it. One conjecture, and the most reasonable and plausible one, is that if Hemmingway had made a full confession it might have involved not only some men who were prominent and influential, but perhaps the Democratic State organization as well. For it was a well-known fact that in 1875 nearly every Democratic club in the State was converted into an armed military company. To fully organize, equip, and arm such a large body of men required an outlay of a large sum of money.   The money was evidently furnished by some persons or through some organization.   Those who raised the money, or who caused it to be raised, no doubt had an eye to the main chance.   A patriotic desire to have the State redeemed (?) was not with them the actuating motive.   When the redemption (?) of the State was an accomplished fact they, no doubt, felt that they were entitled to share in the fruits of that redemption.   Their idea evidently was that the State should be made to pay for its own salvation and redemption, but the only way in which this could be done was to have the people's money in the State treasury appropriated for that purpose otherwise than by legislative enactment.   This, as I have already stated, is only a conjecture, but, under the circumstances, it is the most reasonable and plausible one that can be imagined.

The case of Treasurer Hemmingway is conclusive evidence that in point of efficiency, honesty and official integrity the Democratic party had no advantage over the party that was placed in power chiefly through the votes of colored men.   What was true of Mississippi in this respect was also true, — in a measure, at least,— of the other reconstructed States.

CHAPTER XVII

Although the action of the returning boards in South Carolina, Louisiana, and Florida, gave Mr. Hayes a majority of one vote in the Electoral College, the Democrats, who were largely in the majority in the National House of Representatives, were evidently not willing to acquiesce in the declared result,— claiming that Mr. Tilden had been fairly elected and that he ought to be inaugurated.

Hon. Henry Watterson, of Kentucky,— who was at that time a member of the House,— delivered a fiery speech in which he declared that a hundred thousand armed men would march to Washington to see that Mr. Tilden was inaugurated.   The situation for a while looked very grave.   It seemed as if there would be a dual government, Hayes and Tilden each claiming to be the legally elected President.   To prevent this was the problem then before Congress and the American people.   Conferences, composed of influential men of both parties, were being frequently held in different parts of the city.

The creation of an electoral commission to pass upon and decide the disputed points involved was finally suggested, and was accepted by a majority of both parties. The name of the originator of this suggestion has never been made public; but it is believed by many that Senator Edmunds, of Vermont, was the man, since he was the principal champion of the measure in the Senate. Subsequent events appeared to indicate that Hon. Wm. M. Evarts of New York, was also an influential party to the scheme, if not the originator of it. At any rate, no one seemed to have been sufficiently proud of it to lay claim to its paternity. It was merely a temporary scheme, intended to tide over an unpleasant, and perhaps dangerous, condition which existing remedies did not fully meet. It was equivalent to disposing of the Presidency by a game of chance,— for the composition of the proposed commission was, politically, purely a matter of chance.

As finally agreed upon, the measure provided for a commission to be composed of fifteen members,— five from the House, five from the Senate, and five Justices of the Supreme Court. As the Democrats had a majority in the House, it was agreed that they should have three, and the Republicans two of the five members of that body. Since the Republicans had a majority in the Senate it was agreed that they should have three, and the Democrats two of the five members of that body. Of the five justices of the Supreme Court, two were to be Republicans and two, Democrats; the fifth Justice to be an independent,— or one who was as near an independent as could be found on the bench of that Court.

When the bill creating this commission came before the House I spoke against it, and voted against it, for two reasons. In the first place, I believed it was a dangerous precedent to subject the Presidency of the United States to such a game of chance as was contemplated by the bill then under consideration. Either Hayes or Tilden had been elected, and the result ought to be ascertained according to legal forms. In the second place, I had a suspicion that it was the outgrowth of an understanding or agreement which would result in the abandonment of Southern Republicans by the National Administration.

Mr. Lamar, for instance, did not hesitate to declare that it was more important that the South should have local self-government than that the President should be a Democrat. In other words, what Southern Democrats wanted was to be let alone,— was to have the National Administration keep its hands off, and allow them to manage their own affairs in their own way, even if that way should result in a virtual nullification, in part at least, of the War Amendments to the Federal Constitution.

I had a suspicion that this concession had been granted upon condition that the southern Democratic leaders in Congress would consent to the creation of the proposed commission, and to the ratification of its decision, whatever that decision might be. To such a bargain I did not care to be even an innocent party. My suspicions were strengthened by the fact that the principal opposition among Democrats to the creation of the commission and to the ratification of its decision came from northern Democrats. Southern Democrats, with a few notable exceptions, not only favored the creation of the commission and the ratification of its decision, but even the fiery Watterson was induced to hold his peace and to give expression to his righteous indignation through the medium of a silent vote. That my suspicions were well founded subsequents events more than demonstrated. I took the position that Mr. Hayes had been legally elected, at least according to the forms of law and in the manner prescribed by the Constitution,— and that he should, therefore, be duly inaugurated even if it should be necessary for President Grant, as Commander-in-chief of the Army, to use the military force of the Government for that purpose. I contended that, having been thus legally elected, Hayes should not be subjected to the chance of losing his title to the office and that the incoming President should not be bound by any ante-inauguration pledges, which, in the opinion of some, would have a tendency to cast a cloud upon his title to the office. But the bill was passed and the commission was duly appointed.

At this point the game of chance turned in favor of the Republicans. It was generally understood that Justice David Davis, of Illinois, would be the fifth Justice to be placed on the commission. He was said to be an Independent,— the only member of the Supreme Court that could be thus classed politically. But, in point of fact, he was more of a Democrat than an Independent. Had he been made a member of the commission it is more than probable that Mr. Tilden, and not Mr. Hayes, would have been made President. The Legislature of Illinois was at that time engaged in an effort to elect a United States Senator. The Legislature was composed of about an equal number of Republicans and Democrats,— three Independents holding the balance of power. The Independents at length presented the name of Justice David Davis as their choice for Senator. In order to make sure of the defeat of a Republican, the Democrats joined the Independents in the support of Justice Davis, which resulted in his election. This took place only a few days before the time appointed for the selection of the commissioners.

As soon as it was announced that Justice Davis had been elected to the Senate the Republican leaders in Congress insisted that he was no longer eligible to a seat on the Electoral Commission. This was at first strongly combated by the Democrats, who contended that the Justice was only a Senator-elect, and that he did not cease to be a member of the Court until he tendered his resignation as such; this he was neither required nor expected to do until shortly before the beginning of his term as a Senator. But the Republicans pressed their objections so strongly that the Democrats were induced to yield the point, and Justice Bradley was selected as the fifth Justice. Next to Davis, Bradley came as near being an Independent as any member of the Court. Although he had been appointed as a Republican by President Grant,— as had Justice Davis by President Lincoln,— yet he had rendered several decisions which gave the Democrats hope that he might give the deciding vote in their favor and thus make Mr. Tilden President. In this they were disappointed; for it turned out that the substitution of Bradley for Davis made Hayes President of the United States. It would, perhaps, be unfair to say that the decisions of the commission were rendered regardless of the evidence, the law, and the arguments, yet it so happened that every important point was decided by a strict party vote,— eight to seven.

In this connection it will not be out of place to refer to a scene that was created on the Democratic side of the House by Hon. Ben. Hill, of Georgia. Mr. Hill entered the House one afternoon, having just returned from the Supreme Court Chamber, where the commission was in session. He remarked to one of his colleagues in a low tone that he had just returned from where the sessions of the commission were being held, and that while there the important and valuable information had been imparted to him that on a most vital point the Democrats could with absolute certainty depend upon the vote of Mr. Justice Bradley.

"Can that be possible?" exclaimed his excited and highly elated colleague.

"Yes," replied Mr. Hill, "there can be no doubt about it. I know whereof I speak. It came to me through a source that cannot be questioned."

"Then wait until I can call several of our friends," replied his colleague, "I want them to hear the good news at the same time it is heard by me, so that we can rejoice together."

Mr. Hill was soon surrounded by an eager, excited, and interested group of anxious Democratic members. "We are now ready," said his delighted colleague, whose face was covered with a smile of satisfaction, "to hear the good news."

"Well," replied Mr. Hill, whose manner was grave and whose countenance gave every evidence of deep emotion, "whenever a motion to adjourn is made by a Democratic member of the commission we can safely depend upon the vote of Mr. Justice Bradley being cast in the affirmative."

The heads of the anxious group immediately fell in deep disappointment and despair. But, of course, they did not fail to see the irony of Mr. Hill's remark. It did transpire that whenever a motion to adjourn was made by a Democratic member of the commission it was usually carried by a vote of eight to seven,— Mr. Justice Bradley voting in the affirmative with the Democrats. On no other question, however, could they depend on his vote.

The decision of the Electoral Commission was finally rendered in favor of Mr. Hayes by a strict party vote,— eight to seven. Strong and bitter opposition to the approval of the decision was made in the House by quite a number of northern Democrats, but the majority of southern Democrats, aided by such northern Democrats as represented districts having large commercial interests,— interests that are at all times willing to pay any price for peace,— accepted the decision, and Mr. Hayes was allowed to be peacefully inaugurated.

CHAPTER XVIII

ATTITUDE OF THE HAYES ADMINISTRATION TOWARD THE SOUTH

The new administration had been in power only a short while before it became apparent to southern Republicans that they had very little to expect from this administration. It was generally understood that a southern man would be made Postmaster General in the new cabinet, but it was assumed, of course, by those, at least, who were not fully informed about the secret deals and bargains that had been entered into as a condition precedent to a peaceable inauguration of the new administration, — that he would be a Republican.

Senator Alcorn, of my own State, Mississippi, who had just retired from the Senate, had an ambition to occupy that position. I was one to whom that fact was made known. I did not hesitate to use what little influence I had to have that ambition gratified. I was so earnest and persistent in pressing his claims and merits upon those who were known to be close to the appointing power, that I succeeded in finding out definitely and authoritatively the name of the man that had been agreed upon and would, no doubt, be appointed to that position.   Ex-Senator Key, a Democrat from Tennessee, was the man.   When I informed Senator Alcorn of that fact the manifestation of surprise, disappointment, and disgust with which he received it can better be imagined than described. This was not due so much to the fact that some other one than himself had been selected, but to the fact that the fortunate man was a Southern Democrat.   For the first time the Senator became convinced that southern Republicans had been made the subjects of barter and trade in the shuffle for the Presidency, and that the sacrifice of southern Republicans was the price that had to be paid for the peaceable inauguration of Mr. Hayes. This, in Senator Alcorn's opinion, meant that the Republican party in the reconstructed States of the South was a thing of the past.   There was no hope for it in the future.

"It would have been far better," said the Senator, "not only for the Republican party at the South but for the country at large, to have allowed the Democrats to inaugurate Tilden, and to have taken charge of the Government, than to have purchased Republican victory at such a fearful cost. What inducement can a southern white man now have for becoming a Republican?   Under the present state of things he will be hated at home, and despised abroad.   He will be rejected by his old

friends and associates, and discountenanced by his
new ones. He will incur the odium, and merit the
displeasure and censure of his former friends, associates, and companions with no compensating ad-
vantages for the sacrifices thus made."

The Senator spoke with deep feeling. He could
see that his efforts to build up a strong Republican
party at the South must necessarily fail under such
conditions, and that it was useless to make any
further effort in that direction. Under his influence and leadership very many of the best and most
influential white men in his state had identified
themselves with the Republican party. His efforts
in that direction would have been continued, in
spite of the temporary defeat of the party at the
polls, however severe that defeat might have been,
if those efforts had been appreciated and appropri-
ately recognized by the national leaders of the organization. But when he saw that not only was
this not to be done, but that one of those who was
known to be fully identified with the political per-
secutors of southern Republicans was to be recognized,— thus placing the stamp of approval upon
their work by an administration that was supposed
to be Republican and therefore opposed to such
methods,— it was time for southern white men,
who had been acting with the Republican party and
for those who may have such action in contemplation, to stop and seriously consider the situation.

It was now in order for each one of them to ask himself the question: "Can I afford to do this?"

The appointment of a southern Democrat to a seat in the Cabinet of a Republican President, especially at that particular time, was a crushing blow to southern Republicans. It was the straw that broke the camel's back. Senator Alcorn was a man suitable in every way for the office of Postmaster-General. He had a commanding presence, he was an eloquent speaker, and an able debater,— by nature a leader and not a follower. He had taken an active part in the politics of his state before and after the War. After he identified himself with the Republican party he was ambitious to be chiefly instrumental in building up a strong party in his State and throughout the South which would not only recognize merit in the colored people and accord absolute justice and fair play to them, but which would include in its membership a large percentage, if not a majority, of the best and most substantial white men of that section.

That he had made splendid progress along those lines cannot be denied. The announced southern policy of the Hayes administration not only completed the destruction of what had been thus accomplished, but it made any further progress in that direction absolutely impossible. The selection of ex-Senator Key was, however, not the only

Cabinet appointment which clearly indicated the southern policy of the administration. There were two others,— those of William M. Evarts and Carl Schurz. Those men had been prominent in their bitter opposition to the southern policy of President Grant. Mr. Schurz had been one of the leaders in the Greeley movement against President Grant and the Republican party in 1872, while Mr. Evarts was later the principal speaker at a public indignation meeting that was held at New York to denounce the southern policy of the Grant administration. In fact, John Sherman was the only one of the Cabinet ministers that had a positive national standing, and even his brilliant star was somewhat marred on account of the impression that, as one of the Hayes managers, he had been a party to the deals and agreements that had been made and entered into as a condition precedent to the peaceable induction of Mr. Hayes into office. It was known, or at any rate believed, that Mr. Sherman's appointment as Secretary of the Treasury was for the one specific purpose of bringing about the resumption of specie payments. He was the author of the act which fixed the date when specie payments should be resumed. He had the reputation of being one of the ablest financiers the country had produced. That he should be named to carry into effect the act of which he was the author was to be expected. For the reasons above stated, it was the one Cabinet appointment that met with general approval.

It was soon seen, however, that the Cabinet was so constructed as to make it harmonize with the southern policy of the administration. It was not long before the announcement was officially made in prolix sentences, of which Secretary Evarts was no doubt the author, that the army could not and would not be used to uphold and sustain any State Government in an effort to maintain its supremacy and enforce obedience to its mandates. In other words, it was a public announcement of the fact that if there should be an armed revolt in a State against the lawful State Government which would be strong enough to seize and take possession of that government, the National Government would refuse to interfere, even though a request for assistance should be made by the Chief Executive of the State in the manner and form prescribed by the Constitution. I have never believed that this policy,— which was meant, of course, for the South,— was in harmony with Mr. Hayes' personal convictions; especially in view of his public utterances during the progress of the campaign and immediately after the announcement had been made that he had been defeated. But he no doubt asked himself the question: "What can I do?" This is what he had been bound to do, by his managers through the medium of an ante-inauguration pledge, which he felt in honor bound to respect. Mr. Hayes was not a man of sufficient force of character to disregard and repudiate such a pledge or bargain. Had he been a Napoleon, or even an Andrew Jackson, he would have declared that no man or set of men had any authority to make for him any ante-inauguration pledge, promise, or bargain by which he would be bound as chief magistrate of the country. To the contrary, he would have openly and publicly declared:

"I am President, or I am not. That I am the legally elected President is a recognized and undisputed fact, and, as such, I shall neither recognize nor respect any pledge, promise or bargain which involves dishonor on my part or acquiescence in the suspension, violation or evasion of the Constitution or of any law made in pursuance thereof. As President of the United States I have taken and subscribed to an oath by which I am bound to uphold the Constitution of my country, and to see that the laws are duly executed and enforced. That oath I am determined to respect and honor. I shall not only do all in my power to see that the Constitution and the laws of the land are obeyed and enforced,— both in letter and in spirit,— but it is also my determination to see that every American citizen is protected in the exercise and enjoyment of his rights, as far as it may be in the power of the President to protect him." Such a declaration, accompanied by an honest effort to carry the same into effect, even if he had been unsuccessful, would have carried the name of R. B. Hayes down in history as one of the greatest and most brilliant statesmen our country had ever produced. But, he was not equal to the occasion, and therefore failed to take advantage of such a golden opportunity. On the contrary, he decided to live up to and carry out to the very letter, every pledge, promise, agreement or bargain that had been made in his behalf, which involved the dishonor of his own name and the disgrace of his country. Packard, for Governor of Louisiana, and Chamberlain, for Governor of South Carolina, were voted for at the same time that the Hayes electors were voted for in their respective States. Each of these candidates polled a much larger vote than that of the Hayes electors. If, therefore, Mr. Hayes was legally or mortally entitled to the electoral votes of those States, without which he could not have been elected, those men were entitled to be recognized and supported as Governor of their respective States. But it was a well-known fact that without the support and backing of the National Administration at that particular time, they could not maintain and enforce their authority against the organization of the Democratic party. The public announcement of the southern policy of the National Administration put an effectual end to any further effort on the part of either Packard or Chamberlain. The Administration not only deserted and abandoned those two men and the party for which they had so bravely and so gallantly stood, but it allowed the very men whose votes made Mr. Hayes President to be harassed and persecuted for what they had done in that direction. After Packard surrendered to the inevitable he was tendered a position in the foreign service, which he accepted. When Chamberlain was forced to abandon the hopeless struggle in South Carolina, he moved to New York and engaged in the practice of law. Politically he affiliated with the Democratic party until his death.

CHAPTER XIX

Mr. Blaine had been elected to the United States Senate from Maine, his term beginning March 4th, 1877. The term for which Mr. Lamar, of Mississippi, had been elected, commenced at the same time. It was not possible to have a Congressional investigation of the Mississippi election of 1875 unless the same should be ordered by the Senate,—the Republicans having a small majority in that body. Each House being the sole judge of the elections and qualifications of its own members, the Senate could, of course, have Mr. Lamar's credentials referred to the Committee of Privileges and Elections, with instructions to make an investigation of the methods used to carry the election. This committee would ascertain and report whether or not there had been a legal and valid election in that State, and, pending the investigation and report by the committee and the disposition of the same by the Senate, the seat to which Mr. Lamar had been elected would remain vacant. As the result of a number of conferences between Republican Senators and representative Mississippi Republicans, this course was decided upon as the one to be pursued. But, in order to do this, the Senate must have something upon which to base its contemplated action. It could not be expected to take official notice of rumors or newspaper reports of what had taken place. It was therefore decided that a memorial should be drawn up and signed by a number of reputable and well-known citizens of the State, making specific allegations with reference to that election, and concluding with a request that a thorough investigation be made before the Senator, chosen by the Legislature that had been brought into existence by that election, could be admitted to the Senate.

In support of this contemplated action there had been a number of precedents,— the recent case of Mr. Pinchback, of Louisiana, being one of them. It fell to my lot to draw up the memorial. It was to be presented to the Senate and championed in that body by Senator Morton, of Indiana. The Republican majority in the Senate was small. The Democrats, of course, would bitterly oppose the Morton motion. To make sure of its adoption the affirmative vote of nearly every Republican Senator was necessary. At any rate there could be no serious defection in the Republican ranks, otherwise the Morton proposition could not prevail.

That anyone on the Republican side would oppose it was not anticipated, for every one that had been approached expressed his intention of supporting it. No one of the newly elected Senators had been approached. It was not deemed necessary. It was not anticipated that any one of them would do otherwise than support the program that had been agreed upon by the older members of the Senate. Senator Morton was to submit the memorial and make the motion when the name of Mr. Lamar was called to take the oath of office.

The names of the States were called in alphabetical order, about three being called at a time. Maine was reached before Mississippi, and Mr. Blaine was duly sworn in as a Senator from that State. No one expected that he would do otherwise than support the program that had been agreed upon, but, contrary to expectations, as soon as Mississippi was called Mr. Blaine was on his feet, demanding recognition. Of course he was recognized by the chair. He made a motion that Mr. Lamar be sworn in *prima facie* as the Senator from Mississippi. His contention was that, since his credentials were regular, the Senator-elect should be sworn in; and if there should be any question about the legality of the election it could be made the subject of a subsequent investigation.

This unexpected action on the part of Mr. Blaine

took everyone by surprise, with the possible exception of Mr. Lamar, who, no doubt, was well aware of what was in contemplation. It produced consternation and caused a panic among the Republican leaders in the Senate. Hurried and excited conferences were being held while the subject was being debated. For the seriousness of the situation was recognized. Mr. Blaine's defection meant the defeat of the Morton motion should it be made, and the adoption of the Blaine motion by the solid vote of the Democrats, to which would be added a small minority of the Republicans. This division in the ranks of the party at the beginning of the Hayes administration had to be avoided if possible. That Mr. Blaine should recede from his position was, of course, out of the question. Nothing, therefore, remained to be done but for Senator Morton to refrain from making his motion; for a hurried canvass of the Senate had revealed the fact that the motion, if made and brought to a vote, would be defeated, and the effect of such a defeat would be worse than if the motion had not been made. So the Blaine motion was allowed to go by default, and Mr. Lamar was duly sworn in as a Senator from Mississippi. Of course it was well known at the time by many,— Mr. Blaine among the number,— that this ended the controversy and that no subsequent investigation would be made.

That Mr. Blaine was sadly and seriously disappointed at the result of his action in this case, as well as in his action in defeating the Federal Elections Bill, will be made clear in subsequent chapters.

CHAPTER XX

Since the indications were that the Democrats
would be successful in the Congressional elections of 1878, the election in the " shoe-string district " that year was allowed to go by default.

In 1880, the year of the Presidential election, I
decided that I would again measure arms with
Chalmers for Representative in Congress from that
district. It was practically a well-settled fact that
there was to be a bitter fight for the Republican
Presidential nomination that year. There were
three prominent candidates in the field for the nomination,— James G. Blaine, U. S. Grant, and John
Sherman. Grant was especially strong with southern Republicans, while Blaine had very little support
in that section. Sherman was well thought of on
account of the splendid record he had made as a
member of the United States Senate, and, in addition to that, he had the influence and the support of the National Administration, of which he
was a member,— being at that time Secretary of
the Treasury.

In the State of Mississippi Bruce, Hill and I,— the three leading colored men,— had formed an offensive and defensive alliance. Bruce was United States Senator, which position he had secured largely through the influence and active support of myself and Hill,— of Hill especially, since he was on the ground at the time of the election, which enabled him to take personal charge of the campaign before the Legislature in the interest of Mr. Bruce.

Hill had been elected Secretary of State on the ticket with Ames in 1873 and, after the expiration of his term, was, through the influence and support of Bruce and myself, made Collector of Internal Revenue for the State of Mississippi. The office of Secretary of State, to which he was elected in 1873, was one that the Democrats did not take possession of in 1876. Unlike the Governor and Lieutenant-Governor, the removal of the incumbent was not necessary to put that party in possession of the State Government.

I, Lynch, was at that time a member of the National House of Representatives, which position I was able to retain for a long time with the active assistance and support of Bruce and Hill,— especially of Bruce.

That we three should work in perfect political harmony was both natural and proper, since, in doing so, we protected our own interests and secured for ourselves, and for our friends and supporters, appropriate official recognition. At nearly every State convention either Bruce or I was made chairman of the convention, with Hill as floor manager.

The State committee was organized and controlled in the same way. Through that thorough and effective organization I was Chairman of the Republican State Committee from 1881 to 1892, and I could have retained it longer had I consented to serve; notwithstanding the dissolution of the combination, which took place about that time, as will be shown and explained later.

There was a faction in the party that was opposed to the leadership of these three influential colored men, but it was never strong enough to organize or control a State Convention as long as we three worked in union. While this union had the effect of keeping us at the front as recognized leaders of the party it could not be said it was detrimental to the party organization, for the reason that under that leadership the organization never failed to support the men that the party believed to be the strongest. In other words, while we used the party machinery to prevent our own political extinction we never allowed our own ambitions to conflict with what was believed by other influential members of the party to be for the best interest of the organization.

It looked for a while as if the State Convention of 1880 would result in a dissolution of this combination which had so successfully controlled the party organization in the State so many years. Bruce and Hill were supporters of Secretary Sherman for the Republican Presidential nomination, while I was favorable to the candidacy of ex-President Grant. That Grant was the choice of a large majority of the Republicans of the State could not be truthfully denied. Mr. Bruce was the Republican United States Senator in harmony with the administration. Mr. Hill was an office-holder under that administration, and Secretary Sherman was believed to be the administration candidate for the nomination.

As soon as the fact was developed that Bruce and Hill were for Sherman and that I was for Grant, the faction which had always opposed and fought the leadership of the Bruce-Lynch-Hill combination took up the fight for Grant, with the determination to take advantage of Grant's strength and popularity in order to secure control of the party machinery. It was this that prevented at that time a dissolution of the Bruce-Hill-Lynch combination. The situation with which we were confronted made it necessary for the three to come together and, in a spirit of concession, agree upon a common line of action. Upon the suggestion of Mr. Bruce a conference soon took place at which

I agreed that, since it was my purpose to be a candidate for the Congressional nomination in the Sixth or " shoe-string district," I would not be a candidate for delegate to the National Convention, but that I would support Bruce and Hill as delegates from the State at large, with the understanding that, if at any time Sherman's name should be withdrawn and Grant's nomination were possible, they should support Grant.   It was further agreed that I should support the Bruce-Lynch-Hill combination in the fight for the organization of the State Convention, but that I should be at liberty to use my influence for the election of Grant men as delegates other than Bruce and Hill.

At the conclusion of this conference I made public announcement of the fact that, since it was my purpose to become a candidate for Congress in the Sixth or " shoe-string district," I would not be a candidate for delegate to the National Convention but would give my support to Bruce and Hill, for two of the four places on the delegation from the State at large, with the understanding that the delegation, if controlled by them, would not be hostile to Grant.   I had reasons to know that Mr. Bruce, in consequence of his cordial relations with Senator Conkling,— the national leader of the Grant forces, — was not unfriendly to Grant, and that he would use his influence to prevent the delegation from going into any combination for the sole purpose of defeating the nomination of Grant. In other words, Grant was Bruce's second choice for the nomination.

The fight for the delegation was waged with a good deal of heat and bitterness. The canvass had not progressed very far before it was developed that Grant was much stronger than the faction by which he was being supported. The fight was so bitter, and the delegates to the State Convention were so evenly divided, that the result was the election of a compromise delegation which was about evenly divided between Grant and Sherman. Bruce and Hill were among those that were elected.

The National Convention, which was held in Chicago in June of that year, was one of the most exciting and interesting in the history of the party. It was that convention that abolished what was known as " the unit rule." Up to that time the right of a State Convention to elect all the delegates to which the State was entitled,— district as well as State,— and to instruct them as a body had never before been questioned. New York, as well as other States, had instructed the delegates to cast the entire vote of the State for Grant. This was the unit rule. It is a rule which even now is enforced in National Conventions of the Democratic party. It was through the enforcement of this rule that Mr. Cleveland was renominated, when he was so bitterly opposed by a portion of the delegation from

his own State,— especially the Tammany delegates,
— that General Bragg was moved to make the celebrated declaration that he " loved Mr. Cleveland on
account of the enemies he had made." Notwithstanding the fact that those delegates were strongly
opposed to Mr. Cleveland, and though they protested against having their votes recorded for him,
they were so recorded through the application and
enforcement of the unit rule. It was the enforcement of this rule upon which Mr. Conkling insisted
in the National Republican Convention of 1880.
About twenty of the New York district delegates,
under the leadership of Judge W. H. Robertson,
refused to be governed by the instructions of the
State Convention. Their contention was that the
State Convention had no right to bind by instructions any delegates except the four from the State
at large. After a lengthy and heated debate the
convention finally sustained this contention, and
since that time the unit rule has not been recognized in a National Republican Convention.

This action, no doubt, resulted in the defeat of
General Grant for the nomination; for it was a
well-known fact that his nomination was possible
only through the enforcement of the unit rule. His
friends and supporters, however, under the leadership of Senator Conkling, made a strong and desperate fight with the hope that the tide might
ultimately turn in their favor, but with the inten-

tion, in any event, of preventing if possible the nomination of Mr. Blaine.   General Grant's name was placed before the Convention by Senator Conkling in one of his most eloquent and masterly efforts.

"The man whose name I shall place in nomination," he said, " does not hail from any particular State; he hails from the United States.   It is not necessary to nominate a man that can carry Michigan.   Any Republican can carry Michigan.   You should nominate a man that can carry New York. That man is U. S. Grant."

Mr. Blaine's name was placed in nomination by a delegate from Michigan by the name of Joy.   His effort did not come up to public expectation.   The eloquent speech of Senator Frye, of Maine, who seconded the nomination, made up in part for the public disappointment in Mr. Joy's effort.   The name of Secretary John Sherman was placed before the Convention in one of General Garfield's most powerful and convincing efforts.   It is safe to say that the speech delivered by General Garfield on that occasion made him the nominee of that convention. After drawing an eloquent and vivid picture of the kind of man that should be made President,— with the intention of naming John Sherman as the man thus described,— he asked in a tone of voice that was pitched in a high key:

" Who is that man? "

The response came from different parts of the hall, " Garfield."

And sure enough it was Garfield.   After a number of fruitless ballots it became apparent that neither of the three leading candidates could possibly be nominated.   Very few, if any, of the Grant men would at any time go to either Blaine or Sherman.   Very few, if any, of the Sherman men would go to Blaine, while Blaine men could not in any considerable numbers, be induced to go either to Grant or Sherman.   While a number of Sherman men would have supported Grant in preference to Blaine, there were not enough of them, even with the Grant men, to constitute a majority.   When Garfield's name was suggested as a compromise candidate he was found to be acceptable to both the Blaine and the Sherman men as well as to some of the Grant men, who had abandoned all hope of Grant's nomination.   The result was that Garfield was finally made the unanimous choice of the convention.   The New York delegation, being allowed to name the man for Vice-President, nominated Chester A. Arthur, of that State.

Although General Garfield was nominated as a compromise candidate his election was by no means a foregone conclusion.   The Democrats had nominated a strong and popular man, General W. S. Hancock, one of the most brilliant and successful generals in the Union Army.   Associated on the ticket with him was a popular Indiana Democrat, William H. English. It looked for a while as if Democratic success were reasonably certain, especially after the September State and Congressional elections in the State of Maine, the result of which was virtually a Democratic victory.

What was known as the celebrated Mentor Conference then took place. Mentor was the home of General Garfield. The conference consisted of General Garfield, General Grant, and Senator Conkling. Who was instrumental in bringing that conference into existence perhaps will never be known, and what was actually said and done on that occasion will, no doubt, remain a mystery. But it resulted in bringing the Grant-Conkling wing of the party,— which up to that time had been lukewarm and indifferent,— into the active and aggressive support of the ticket. Senator Conkling immediately took the stump and made a brilliant and successful campaign, not only in New York but also in the other close and doubtful States. The result was that Garfield carried New York by a majority of about twenty thousand and was elected. Without New York he would have been defeated; for the South this time was unquestionably solid in its support of the Democratic ticket; at least, according to the forms of law. It was not necessary to resort to the questionable expedient of an electoral commission to determine the

result of that election.   It is safe to say that, but
for the active support given the ticket in that campaign by General Grant and Senator Conkling, New
York would have been lost to the party and Garfield
would have been defeated.   With the election of
Garfield the National House of Representatives
was also Republican.   The majority was small, but
it was large enough to enable the party to organize
the House.   The Garfield administration started
out under very favorable auspices.   How it ended
will be told in another chapter.

CHAPTER XXI

STORY OF THE MISUNDERSTANDING BETWEEN
GARFIELD AND CONKLING

The Garfield Administration, as I have said, started out under most favorable auspices. Mr. Conkling took an active part in the Senate as a champion and spokesman of the administration. He seemed to have taken it for granted, that,— although his bitter enemy, Mr. Blaine, was Secretary of State,— his own influence with the administration would be potential. In conversation with his personal friends he insisted that this was a part of the agreement that had been entered into at the famous Mentor Conference, about which so much had been said and published. If it were true that Mr. Conkling's control of the Federal patronage in New York in the event of Republican success was a part of that agreement, it transpired that Mr. Blaine had sufficient influence with the President to bring about its repudiation.

It is a fact well known that the President was anxious to avoid a break with Senator Conkling. Judge W. H. Robertson, who was a candidate for the Collectorship of the port of New York was

strongly supported by Mr. Blaine.   Judge Robertson had been one of the influential leaders of the
Blaine movement in New York.   It was he who
had disregarded the action of the State Convention
in instructing the delegates to cast the vote of the
State as a unit for General Grant.   In bolting the
action of the State Convention Judge Robertson
carried about nineteen other delegates with him over
to Mr. Blaine.   Therefore Mr. Blaine insisted upon
the appointment of Judge Robertson to the Collectorship of the port at New York.   Senator
Conkling would not consent under any circumstances to this appointment.   Mr. Blaine, it appears, succeeded in convincing the President that,
but for Judge Robertson's action, his, Garfield's,
nomination would have been impossible and that
consequently it would be base ingratitude not to
appoint Robertson to the position for which he was
an applicant.   Mr. Blaine contended that the administration would not only be guilty of ingratitude
should it refuse to appoint his candidate, but that it
would thereby allow itself to be the medium
through which this man was to be punished for
his action in making the existence of the administration possible.

"Can you, Mr. President, afford to do such a
thing as this?" asked Mr. Blaine.

To which the President gave a negative answer.
Perhaps it did not occur to Mr. Blaine at that time

that, while the action of Judge Robertson may have made the nomination of Mr. Garfield possible, the subsequent action of Senator Conkling made his election possible. But, notwithstanding this, the President decided that Judge Robertson should have the office for which he was an applicant.

As previously stated, however, the President was anxious to avoid a break with Senator Conkling. To get the Senator to consent to the appointment of Judge Robertson was the task the President had before him. With that end in view the President invited Mr. Conkling to a private conference, at which he expressed a willingness to allow the New York Senator to name every important Federal officer in New York except the Collector of the Port, if he would consent to the appointment of Judge Robertson to that office. But the only concession Senator Conkling was willing to make was to give his consent to the appointment of Judge Robertson to any position in the foreign service. This was not satisfactory, hence the conference was a failure. The President was thus placed in a very disagreeable dilemma, being thus forced, very much against his inclination, to take a decided stand in a very unpleasant controversy. He was thus forced to choose between Mr. Blaine, his own Secretary of State, on one side, and Senator Conkling on the other. To one he felt that he was indebted for his nomination. To the other he believed that his election was largely due. It was asserted by some who were in a position to know that, if the President had taken sides with Mr. Conkling, Mr. Blaine would have immediately tendered his resignation, and thus would have severed his official connection with the administration. While no intimation of this was made known to the President, yet he no doubt believed, in consequence of the deep and intense interest Mr. Blaine had shown in the matter, that such action on his part, in the event of an adverse decision, was more than probable. When the President saw that there was no escape,— that he was obliged to take a decided stand one way or the other,— he decided to sustain the contention of his Secretary of State. Consequently, after the fruitless conference between the President and Senator Conkling, the name of Judge Robertson for Collector of the port at New York, was sent to the Senate. Senator Conkling, joined by his colleague, Senator Platt, at first made an effort to have the nomination rejected, but the other Republican Senators were not willing to place themselves in open opposition to the administration. When the fact was developed that the nomination would be confirmed, Senators Conkling and Platt immediately tendered their resignations.

This in my opinion was a grave blunder on their part, as subsequent events more than proved. They had before them the example of Senator Sumner, by which they should have profited. Senator Sumner was greatly humiliated, when, through the influence of the administration, he was supplanted by Senator Cameron as Chairman of the Senate Committee on Foreign Relations on account of a misunderstanding with President Grant, growing out of the effort on the part of the administration to bring about the annexation of Santo Domingo, to which Senator Sumner was bitterly opposed. Yet he did not,— because he was thus, as he felt, unjustly humiliated,— resign his seat in the Senate. He realized that while he was commissioned to speak for his own State, his great power and immense influence were not confined solely to that particular State. He appreciated the fact that when he spoke and voted as a Senator, he did so, not merely as a Senator from the State of Massachusetts, but as a Senator of the United States. He belonged to no one State, but to the United States. He had,— on account of his great intellect, power, influence, and ability,— long since ceased to be the spokesman and representative of any particular State or section; he was a representative of his country — recognized as such throughout the civilized world. Knowing these things to be true Sumner did not feel that he should deprive the people of his valuable services simply because he was not in harmony with the administration upon some one matter, however important that matter might be.   In this Senator Sumner was unquestionably right.

What, then, was true of Senator Sumner was equally true of Senators Conkling and Platt in their misunderstanding with President Garfield about the Collectorship of the port of New York.

Mr. Conkling was one of the greatest men our country had ever produced.   He was a man of much influence and great power.   He was not only an intellectual giant, but he was a man of commanding presence and attractive personality.   As an orator he had few equals and no superiors.   As in the case of Senator Sumner he spoke and voted as a Senator not merely for his State, but for his country; not for any particular section or locality, but for the United States.   He was too great a man, and his services were too important and valuable for his country to be deprived of them merely on account of a misunderstanding between the President and himself about Federal patronage in New York.   He and his colleague should have retained their seats in the Senate and trusted to the judgment of their fellow-citizens for a vindication of their course and action in that as in other matters.   They not only made a mistake in resigning their seats in the Senate, but consummated it when they went before the Legislature of their State, which was then in session, and asked for a vindication through the medium of reëlection.   This was subjecting their friends to a test to which they were not willing to submit. Their friends, both in the Legislature and out of it, were loyal to them, and this loyalty would have been demonstrated at the proper time and in the right way had the two Senators remained in a position which would have enabled their adherents to do so without serious injury to the party organization. But when these men were asked, as the price of their loyalty, to place the party organization in the State in open opposition to the National Administration for no other reason than a misunderstanding about Federal patronage in the city of New York, they did not think that the controversy was worth the price; hence the request was denied. The result was the defeat of Conkling and Platt, and the election of two Administration Republicans, Warner Miller and E. G. Lapham.

This foolhardy act of Conkling's had the unfortunate effect of eliminating him from public life, at least so far as an active participation in public affairs was concerned. But this was not true of Mr. Platt. He was determined to come to the front again, and in this he was successful. At the very next National Convention (1884) he turned up as one of the Blaine delegates from New York, and was one of the speakers that seconded Mr. Blaine's nomination. That was something Mr. Conkling never could have been induced to do. He

THE FACTS OF RECONSTRUCTION 209

was proud, haughty and dictatorial. He would never forget a friend, nor forgive an enemy. To his friends he was loyal and true. To his enemies he was bitter and unrelenting. For his friends he could not do too much. From his enemies he would ask no quarter and would give none. More than one man of national reputation has been made to feel his power, and suffer the consequences resulting from his ill-will and displeasure. But for the unfriendliness of Mr. Conkling, Mr. Blaine no doubt would have attained the acme of his ambition in reaching the Presidency of the United States. It was Mr. Blaine's misfortune to have made an enemy of the one man who, by a stroke of destiny, was so situated as to make it possible for him to prevent the realization of Mr. Blaine's life ambition. It was due more to Mr. Conkling than to any other one man that Mr. Blaine was defeated for the Republican Presidential nomination in 1876,— the year in which he could have been elected had he been nominated.

Mr. Conkling was too much of a party man to support the Democratic ticket under any circumstances, hence, in 1884, when Mr. Blaine was at length nominated for the Presidency, Mr. Conkling gave the ticket the benefit of his silence. That silence proved to be fatal. In consequence of Mr. Conkling's silence and apparent indifference in 1884, Mr. Blaine lost New York, the pivotal State, and was defeated by Mr. Cleveland for the Presidency. The falling off in the Republican vote in Mr. Conkling's home county alone caused the loss of the State and of the Presidency of the United States to the Republican party.

The quarrel between Blaine and Conkling originated when both of them were members of the House of Representatives. In a controversy that took place between them on the floor of the House Mr. Blaine referred to Mr. Conkling as the member from New York with the "turkey gobbler strut." That remark made the two men enemies for life. That remark wounded Mr. Conkling's pride; and he could never be induced to forgive the one who had so hurt him.

As a United States Senator Conkling was both felt and feared. No Senator ever desired to get into a controversy with him, because he was not only a speaker of great power and eloquence, but as a debater he was cutting and scathing in his irony. Senator Lamar, of Mississippi, who as an eloquent orator compared favorably with the best on both sides of the Chamber, had the misfortune to get into a controversy on one occasion with the distinguished New York Senator. In repelling an accusation that the Senator from Mississippi had made against him, Mr. Conkling said: " If it were not that this is the United States Senate I would characterize the member from Mississippi as a coward and a prevaricator."

If those words had been uttered by any other Senator than Roscoe Conkling it is more than probable that he would have been severely reprimanded; no other Senator, however, cared to incur Conkling's displeasure by becoming the author of a resolution for that purpose.

Senator John J. Ingalls, of Kansas, was the only other Senator that ever came near holding a similar position; for, while he was by no means the equal of Conkling, he was both eloquent and sarcastic. For that reason Senators were not anxious to get into a controversy with him. On one occasion it seemed that he came near getting into a dispute with Senator Manderson, of Nebraska. While the Senator from Nebraska was delivering a speech, he made a remark to which the Senator from Kansas took exceptions. When the Kansas Senator arose, — flushed with anger, and laboring under intense excitement,— to correct what he declared in words that were more forcible than elegant, to be a misstatement of his position, the Senator from Nebraska did not hesitate for a moment to accept the correction, remarking by way of explanation and apology that he had not distinctly heard the remark the Senator from Kansas had made, and to which he was alluding when interrupted.

"Then," retorted the Senator from Kansas, "that is your misfortune."

"I admit," the Senator from Nebraska quickly replied, "that it is always a misfortune not to hear the Senator from Kansas."

The unfortunate controversy between President Garfield and Senator Conkling resulted in a national calamity. The bitterness that grew out of it had the effect of bringing a crank on the scene of action. Early in July, 1881,— when the President, in company with Mr. Blaine, was leaving Washington for his summer vacation,— this cowardly crank, who had waited at the railroad station for the arrival of the distinguished party, fired the fatal shot which a few months later terminated the earthly career of a President who was beloved by his countrymen without regard to party or section.

Whatever may have been the merits of this unfortunate controversy, it resulted in the political death of one and the physical death of the other; thus depriving the country of the valuable services of two of the greatest and most intellectual men that our country had ever produced.

When the President died I was at my home, Natchez, Mississippi, where a memorial meeting was held in honor of his memory, participated in by both races and both parties. I had the honor of being one of the speakers on that occasion. That part of my remarks which seemed to attract most attention and made the deepest impression was the declaration that it was my good fortune, as a member of the National House of Representatives, to sit within the sound of his eloquent voice on a certain memorable occasion when he declared that there could never be a permanent peace and union between the North and the South until the South would admit that, in the controversy that brought on the War the North was right and the South was wrong. Notwithstanding that declaration, in which he was unquestionably right, I ventured the opinion that, had he been spared to serve out the term for which he had been elected, those who had voted for him would have been proud of the fact that they had done so, while those who had voted against him would have had no occasion to regret that he had been elected.

Upon the death of President Garfield Vice-President Arthur,— who had been named for that office by Mr. Conkling,— became President; but he, too, soon incurred the displeasure of Mr. Conkling. Mr. Conkling had occasion to make a request of the President which the latter could not see his way clear to grant. For this Mr. Conkling never forgave him. The President tried hard afterwards to regain Mr. Conkling's friendship, but in vain. He even went so far, it is said, as to tender Mr. Conkling a seat on the bench of the Supreme Court; but the tender was contemptuously declined.

President Arthur aspired to succeed himself as President. As a whole he gave the country a splendid administration, for which he merited a renomination and election as his own successor. While there was a strong and well-organized effort to secure for him a renomination, the probabilities are that the attitude of Mr. Conkling towards him contributed largely to his defeat; although the ex-Senator took no active part in the contest. But, as in the case of Mr. Blaine, his silence, no doubt, was fatal to Mr. Arthur's renomination.

CHAPTER XXII

THE NATIONAL CAMPAIGN OF 1884

When the Forty-seventh Congress expired March 4th, 1883, I returned to my home at Natchez, Mississippi. 1884 was the year of the Presidential election. Early in the year it was made clear that there was to be a bitter fight for the Presidential nomination.

President Arthur was a candidate to succeed himself; but Mr. Blaine, it was conceded, would be the leading candidate before the Convention. Senator John Sherman was also a candidate. It was generally believed that Senator Edmunds of Vermont would get a majority of the delegates from the New England States. Mr. Blaine was weaker in his own section, New England, than in any other part of the country except the South. The South, however, had somewhat relented in its opposition to him, as previously stated, in consequence of which he had a stronger support from that section than in any of his previous contests for the nomination; to this fact may be attributed his nomination by the Convention. That support, it was believed, was due more to a deference to public opinion at the North,

— the section that must be depended upon to elect the ticket,— than confidence in Mr. Blaine.

The delegation from my own State, Mississippi, was, with one exception, solid in its support of President Arthur. The one exception was Hon. H. C. Powers, one of the delegates from the first district.

Two active, aggressive, able and brilliant young men had just entered the field of national politics, both of them having been elected delegates to this convention. Those men were Theodore Roosevelt, of New York, and H. C. Lodge, of Massachusetts. Both were vigorously opposed to the nomination of Mr. Blaine. Roosevelt's election as a delegate from New York was in the nature of a national surprise. Mr. Blaine was believed to be very strong in that State. The public, therefore, was not prepared for the announcement that Theodore Roosevelt,— an anti-Blaine man,— had defeated Senator Warner Miller,— the able and popular leader of the Blaine forces in that State,— as delegate to the National Convention from the State at large. The Blaine leaders were brought to a realization of the fact, that, in consequence of their unexpected defeat in New York, it was absolutely necessary, in order to make sure of the nomination of their candidate, to retain the support they had among the Southern delegates.

With that end in view the National Committee, in

which the Blaine men had a majority, selected a Southern man, Hon. Powell Clayton, of Arkansas, for temporary chairman of the Convention. The anti-Blaine men,— under the leadership of Messrs. Roosevelt, Lodge, Hoar, Hanna, Geo. William Curtis and others,— decided to select another Southern man to run against Clayton. For that purpose a conference was held;— composed of many of the active supporters of Arthur, Sherman, and Edmunds,— to select the man to put up against Clayton.

I did not attend the conference. Senator Hoar suggested my name and insisted that I was the man best fitted for the position. After a brief discussion it was decided unanimously to select me. A committee was appointed, of which ex-Governor Pinchback, of Louisiana, was chairman, to wait on me and inform me of what had been done, and to insist upon my acceptance of the distinguished honor which had thus been conferred upon me. Another committee was appointed,— of which Hon. M. A. Hanna, of Ohio, was chairman, to poll the Convention to find out the strength of the movement. This committee subsequently reported that Clayton would be defeated and Lynch elected by a majority of about thirty-five votes. For two reasons I had some doubt about the propriety of allowing my name to be thus used. First, I doubted the wisdom of the movement. It had been the uniform custom to allow the National Committee to select the temporary chairman of the Convention, and I was inclined to the opinion that a departure from that custom might not be a wise step. Second, I did not think it could possibly win. My opinion was that a number of delegates that might otherwise vote for me could not be induced to vote in favor of breaking what had been a custom since the organization of the party.

I did not come to a definite decision until the morning of the day that the Convention was to be organized. Just before that body was called to order I decided to confer with Maj. William McKinley and Hon. M. A. Hanna, of Ohio, and act upon their advice. McKinley was for Blaine and Hanna was for Sherman, but my confidence in the two men was such that I believed their advice would not be influenced by their personal preference for the Presidential nomination. I did not know at that time that Mr. Hanna had taken an active part in the deliberations of the conference that resulted in my selection for temporary chairman of the Convention. I first consulted Major McKinley. I had served with him in Congress and had become very much attached to him. He frankly stated that, since he was a Blaine man, he would be obliged to vote against me, but he told me that this was an opportunity that comes to a man but once in a lifetime.

"If you decline," he said, "the anti-Blaine men will probably put up someone else who would, no doubt, receive the same vote that you would receive. If it is possible for them to elect anyone, I know of no man I would rather have them thus honor than you. While, therefore, I shall vote against you and hope you will not be elected,— simply because I am a Blaine man, and a vote for you means a vote against Blaine,— I shall not advise you to decline the use of your name."

I then approached Mr. Hanna, who appeared to be surprised that I hesitated about consenting to the use of my name.

"We have you elected," he said, "by a majority of about thirty-five. You cannot decline the use of your name, for two reasons; first, since we know we have the votes necessary to elect you, should you now decline the public would never believe otherwise than that you had been improperly influenced. This you cannot afford. In the second place, it would not be treating us fairly. We have selected you in perfect good faith, with the expectation that you would allow your name to be thus used; or, if not, you would have declined in ample time to enable us to reconvene, and select someone else. To decline now, on the eve of the election, when it is impossible for us to confer and agree upon another man for the position, would be manifestly unfair to us as well as to your own candidate for the Presidential nomination, whose chances may be injuriously affected thereby."

This argument was both impressive and effective. I then and there decided to allow my name to be used. I learned afterwards that it was under the direction and management of Mr. Hanna that the Convention had been so carefully and accurately polled. That his poll was entirely correct was demonstrated by the result. This also established the fact that as an organizer Mr. Hanna was a master, which was subsequently proved when he managed Mr. McKinley's campaign both for the nomination and election to the Presidency in 1896.

When the Convention was called to order, and the announcement was made that the National Committee had selected Hon. Powell Clayton, of Arkansas, for temporary chairman of the Convention, an attractive young man in the Massachusetts delegation was recognized by the chair. He gave his name as H. C. Lodge. He said he rose to place the name of another gentleman in nomination; and, after making a neat and appropriate speech in commendation of his candidate,— a speech that created a very favorable impression,— he named ex-Congressman John R. Lynch, of Mississippi, whom he believed to be a suitable man for the position. The ball was then opened. This was an indication of a combination of the field against Blaine. Many speeches were made on both sides, but they were temperate in tone, and free from bitterness. Among those that spoke in support of my candidacy were Messrs. Theodore Roosevelt, and Geo. William Curtis, of New York. When the debate was over the chairman directed that the States be called in alphabetical order,— the roll of delegates from each State to be called, so as to allow each individual delegate to cast his own vote. When Mississippi was reached, I joined with H. C. Powers, the Blaine member of the delegation, in voting for Clayton. The result was just about what Mr. Hanna said it would be.

The Blaine men were discouraged and the anti-Blaine men were jubilant. It was claimed by the latter, and apprehended by the former, that it was indicative of Mr. Blaine's defeat for the nomination. It certainly looked that way, but the result of the election for the temporary chairmanship proved to be misleading. Mr. Hanna's poll was not to find out how many delegates would vote for the nomination of Mr. Blaine, but how many would vote for Lynch for temporary chairman. On that point his poll was substantially accurate. It was assumed that every Blaine man would vote for Mr. Clayton. This is where the mistake was made. It turned out that there were some Blaine men, especially from the South, that voted for Lynch. The result, therefore, was not, as it was hoped it would be, an accurate test of the strength of the Blaine and anti-Blaine forces in the Convention.

Since my election had not been anticipated,— at least, by me,— my speech of acceptance was necessarily brief. I presided over the deliberations of the Convention the greater part of two days, when Hon. John B. Henderson, of Missouri, was introduced as the permanent chairman. This is the same Henderson, who, as a Republican United States Senator from Missouri, voted against the conviction of President Andrew Johnson, who had been impeached by the House of Representatives for high crimes and misdemeanors in office. The Democratic Senators needed but seven votes from the Republican side of the chamber to prevent conviction. They succeeded in getting the exact number, Senator Henderson being one. He appears to have been the only one of that number that politically survived that act. All others soon passed into political oblivion; although several of them subsequently identified themselves with the Democratic party. While it may be said that Senator Henderson survived the act, it is true that his election as a delegate to the National Republican Convention of 1884 and his selection as the permanent chairman thereof are the only prominent illustrations of that fact.

During the deliberations of the Convention Mr. Bishop, one of the delegates from Massachusetts, introduced a resolution to change the basis of representation in future National Conventions of the party. His plan was to make the number of Republican votes cast, counted, certified and returned at the last preceding National election, the basis of representation in succeeding National Conventions.

Hon. W. O. Bradley, of Kentucky, led off in a very able, eloquent, and convincing speech in opposition to the resolution. The colored delegates from the South selected me to present their side of the question. For that purpose I was recognized by the chair, and spoke against the resolution. In the first place I called attention to the fact that if elections were fair, and the official count honest in every State, the probabilities were that there would be no occasion for the proposed change. That the change proposed would result in a material reduction in the representation in future conventions chiefly from Southern States was because the greater part of the Republican votes in some of said States were suppressed by violence or nullified by fraud. The effect of the change proposed would be simply to make such questionable methods the basis of representation in future Republican National Conventions. This, I claimed, the Republican party could not afford to do. At the conclusion of my remarks the resolution was withdrawn by its author, Mr. Bishop, who came over to my seat, and congratulated me upon the way in which I had presented the case; stating at the same time that my speech had convinced him that his proposition was a mistake.

After a hotly contested fight Mr. Blaine was finally nominated. Senator John A. Logan, of Illinois, was named as the candidate for Vice-President. It looked as if the time had at last come when the brilliant statesman from Maine would have the acme of his ambition completely realized.

I was honored by the delegation from my State with being made a member of the National Committee, and also a member of the committee that was named to wait on Mr. Blaine and notify him officially of his nomination. The notification committee went all the way to Mr. Blaine's home, Augusta, Maine, to discharge that duty.

The ceremony of notification took place in Mr. Blaine's front yard. The weather was fine. The notification speech was delivered by the chairman, Senator Henderson, to which Mr. Blaine briefly responded, promising to make a more lengthy reply in the form of a letter of acceptance. At the conclusion of the ceremony he called me to one side and asked what was the outlook in Mississippi. I informed him that he could easily carry the State by a substantial majority if we could have a fair election and an honest count; but that under the existing order of things this would not be possible, and that the State would be returned against him.

" Oh, no," he replied, " you are mistaken about

that.   Mr. Lamar will see that I get a fair count in Mississippi."

I confess that this remark surprised me very much.

" Mr. Blaine," I replied, " you may understand the political situation in Mississippi better than I do, but I know whereof I speak when I say that Mr. Lamar would not if he could and could not if he would, secure you a fair count in Mississippi.   The State will be returned against you."

" You will find," he said, " that you are mistaken.   Mr. Lamar will see that I get a fair count in Mississippi."

Mr. Lamar not only made an aggressive campaign against Mr. Blaine, but it was chiefly through his influence and efforts that the State was returned against Mr. Blaine by a very large majority.   And yet no one who knew Mr. Lamar could justly accuse him of being an ingrate.   He was essentially an appreciative man; as he never failed to demonstrate whenever and wherever it was possible for him to do so.   No one knew better than did Mr. Lamar that he was under deep and lasting obligations to Mr. Blaine; but it seems that with all his wisdom and political sagacity and foresight Mr. Blaine was unable to distinguish between a personal and a political obligation.   Mr. Lamar felt that what Mr. Blaine had done for him was personal, not political, and that if his,—Lamar's,—

party was in any respect the beneficiary thereof, it was merely incidental. At any rate, it was utterly impossible for him to serve Mr. Blaine in a political way. Had he made the effort to do so he not only would have subjected himself to the accusation of party treachery, but it would have resulted in his own political downfall. To expect any ambitious man to make such a sacrifice as this was contrary to human nature.

The truth was that Mr. Blaine had been chiefly instrumental in bringing about a condition of affairs at the South which made it impossible for any of his Democratic or Republican friends in that section to be of any material service to him at the time he most needed them. And yet, he could not see this until it was too late. In spite of this he would have been elected, but for the fact that he lost the pivotal State of New York by a small plurality, about eleven hundred and forty-seven, the reasons for which have been given in a previous chapter. It is therefore sad, but true, that by his own act this able and brilliant statesman, like Henry Clay, died without having reached the acme of his ambition,— the Presidency of the United States.

CHAPTER XXIII

THE ELECTION OF GROVER CLEVELAND

The Republicans of my district insisted that I make the race for Congress again in 1884, and I decided to do so, although I knew it would be useless for me to do so with any hope of being elected, for I knew the prospect of success was not as favorable as two years previous.

Judge Van Eaton, the Democratic candidate for Congressman in 1882, was a representative of the better element, and would, therefore, rather be defeated than be declared elected through the enforcement and application of questionable methods. He publicly declared on several occasions that, as anxious as he was to be a member of Congress, he would rather be defeated than have a certificate of election tainted with fraud. In other words, if he could not be fairly and honestly elected he preferred to be defeated. He insisted upon a fair election and an honest count. This was not agreeable to many of his party associates. They believed and privately asserted that his open declarations on that point not only carried an implied reflection upon his party in connection with previous elections, but that he was taking an unnecessary risk in his own case. Chiefly for these reasons, the Judge, though a strong and able man, was denied the courtesy of a nomination for a second term. It had always been the custom to allow a member to serve at least two terms; but this honor was denied Judge Van Eaton, the nomination being given to Honorable T. R. Stockdale, of Pike county.

Stockdale was a different type of a man from Van Eaton. He was in perfect accord with the dominant sentiment of his party. He felt that he had been nominated to go to Congress,—"peaceably and fairly," if possible, but to go in any event. Then, again, that was the year of the Presidential election, and the Democrats were as confident of success that year as they had been in 1876 and in 1880.

For President and Vice-President the candidates were Blaine and Logan, Republicans, and Cleveland and Hendricks, Democrats.

Mr. Cleveland had the prestige of having been elected Governor of New York by a majority of about one hundred thousand. New York was believed to be the pivotal and the decisive State, and that its votes would determine the election for President. That the Republicans, even with such a popular man as Mr. Blaine as their candidate, would be able to overcome the immense majority by which Mr. Cleveland had carried the State for

Governor was not believed by any Democrat to be possible. The Democrats did not take into account any of the local circumstances that contributed to such a remarkable result; but they were well known to Republicans in and out of that State. One of the principal contributory causes was a determination on the part of thousands of Republican voters in that State to resent at the polls National interference in local State affairs.

Judge Folger, President Arthur's Secretary of the Treasury, was the Republican candidate against Mr. Cleveland for the Governorship when the latter was elected by such an immense majority. It was a well-known fact that Judge Folger could not have been nominated but for the active and aggressive efforts of the National Administration, and of its agents and representatives. The fight for the Republican nomination for Governor that year was the beginning of the bitter fight between the Blaine and the Arthur forces in the State for the delegation in 1884. In the nomination of Judge Folger the Blaine men were defeated. To neutralize the prestige which the Arthur men had thus secured, thousands of the Blaine men, and some who were not Blaine men, but who were against the National Administration for other reasons, refused to vote for Judge Folger, and thus allowed the State to go Democratic by default. In 1884, when Mr. Blaine was the candidate of the Republicans for the Presidency, a sufficient number of anti-Blaine men in New York,— in a spirit of retaliation, no doubt,— pursued the same course and thus allowed the State again to go Democratic by default. The loss which Mr. Blaine sustained in the latter case, therefore, was much greater than that gained by him in the former.

But, let the causes, circumstances, and conditions be what they may, there was not a Democrat in Mississippi in 1884 who did not believe that Mr. Cleveland's election to the Presidency was a foregone conclusion. That he would have the support of the Solid South there was no doubt. Those States, they believed, were as certain to be returned Democratic as the sun would rise on the morning of the day of the election.

Although I accepted the nomination for Congress, I as chairman of the Republican State Committee, devoted the greater part of my time to the campaign throughout the State. Mr. Blaine had many warm friends and admirers among the white men and Democrats in the State, some of them being outspoken in their advocacy of his election. In making up the electoral ticket I made every effort possible to get some of those men to consent to the use of their names. One of them, Joseph N. Carpenter, of my own home town, Natchez, gave his consent to the use of his name. He was one of the solid business men of the town. He was not only a large property owner but the principal owner of a local steamboat that was engaged in the trade on the Mississippi River between Natchez and Vicksburg. He was also the principal proprietor of one of the cotton-seed-oil mills of the town. In fact his name was associated with nearly every important enterprise in that community. Socially no family stood higher than his in any part of the South. His accomplished wife was a Miss Mellen, whose brother, William F. Mellen, was one of the most brilliant members of the bar that the State had ever produced. She had another brother who acquired quite a distinction as a minister of the gospel.

When the announcement was made public that Joseph N. Carpenter was to be an elector on the Republican ticket, intense excitement was immediately created. The Democratic press of the State immediately turned their batteries upon him. Personal friends called upon him in large numbers and urged him to decline. But he had consented to serve, and he felt that it was his duty, and ought to be his privilege to do so. Besides, he was a sincere Blaine man. He honestly believed that the election of Mr. Blaine would be conducive to the best interests of the country, the South especially. To these appeals, therefore, he turned a deaf ear. But it was not long before he was obliged to yield to the pressure. The fact was soon made plain to him that, if he allowed his name to remain on that ticket, the probabilities were that he would be financially ruined. He would soon find that his boat would be without either passengers or freight; his oil mill would probably be obliged to close because there would be no owners of the raw material of whom he could make purchases at any price, and even his children at school would, no doubt, be subjected to taunts and insults, to say nothing of the social cuts to which his family might be subjected. He was, therefore, brought to a painful realization of the fact that he was confronted with conditions which he had not fully anticipated. He could then see, as he had never seen before, that he had been brought face to face with a condition and not a theory. He was thus obliged to make his choice between accepting those conditions upon the one hand, and on the other the empty and temporary honor of serving as an elector on the Blaine Republican ticket. His convictions, his manhood and his self-respect were on one side; his material interests and family obligations were on the other. His mental condition during that period can better be imagined than described. After giving thoughtful consideration and sleepless nights to the matter, he at length decided to yield to the pressure and decline the use of his name. He informed me of his decision through the medium of a private letter which he said he had written with great reluctance and sincere regret. The committee thereupon named Dr. Jackson, of Amite County, an old line Republican, to fill the vacancy.

It will thus be seen that in pursuing a course that Mr. Blaine thought would place southern Democrats under obligations to him he placed a weapon in the hands of his own personal and political enemies by which they were enabled to crush and silence his friends and supporters; for after all it is not so much the love of fair play, as it is the fear of punishment, that actuates the average man in obeying the laws and respecting the rights and privileges of others. Mr. Blaine's friends and supporters at the South were the very people who stood most in need of that security and protection which can come only through a thorough and impartial enforcement of laws for the protection of citizens in the exercise and enjoyment of their civil and political rights, as well as the enforcement of laws for the protection of life, liberty and property.

Judge H. F. Simrall, one of the most brilliant lawyers in the State,— who came into the Republican party under the leadership of General Alcorn in 1869, and who had served as a Justice of the Supreme Court of the State,— made an effort to canvass the State for Mr. Blaine, but his former associates, with whom he tried to reason, treated him with such scanty courtesy that he soon became discouraged and abandoned the effort.

There were two factions in the Democratic party,

Mr. Lamar being the recognized head of one of them. His political enemies suspected and some of them accused him of being partial to Mr. Blaine. To save himself and his friends from humiliation and defeat in his own party it was necessary for him to dispel that suspicion, and disprove those accusations. With that end in view he made a thorough canvass of the State in the interest of Mr. Cleveland and the Democratic party. The State was returned for Mr. Cleveland by a large majority, for which Mr. Lamar was in a great measure credited. Mr. Blaine finally saw his mistake, which he virtually admitted in the speech delivered by him at his home immediately after the election; but it was then too late to undo the mischief that had been done. It was like locking the stable door after the horse had been stolen. That Mr. Blaine died without having attained the goal of his ambition was due chiefly to his lack of foresight, poor judgment, political blunders, and a lack of that sagacity and acumen which are so essential in a successful party leader.

CHAPTER XXIV

In selecting his first cabinet Mr. Cleveland did
Mr. Lamar and the State of Mississippi the honor
of making him his Secretary of the Interior.   Early
in the administration, upon the occasion of my first
visit to Washington after the inauguration of Mr.
Cleveland, I called on Secretary Lamar to pay him
my respects and tender him my congratulations upon
his appointment.   When I entered his office he was
engaged in conversation with some prominent New
York Democrats, Mayor Grace, of New York City,
being one of the party.   The Secretary received
me cordially; and, after introducing me to the gen-
tlemen with whom he was conversing, requested me
to take a seat in the adjoining room, which was used
as his private office, until the departure of the gentle-
men with whom he was then engaged; remarking at
the same time that there was an important matter
about which he desired to talk with me.

I had been seated only a short while before he
made his appearance.   As soon as he had taken his
seat he said:

"Lynch, you have shown me some favors in the past, and I desire to manifest in a substantial way my appreciation of what you have done for me and the friendly interest you have taken in me. No one knows better than I do, or can appreciate more keenly than I can, the value of the services you have rendered me, and the satisfactory results of your friendly interest in me. In saying this I do not wish to even intimate that you have done anything for me that was inconsistent with the position occupied by you as an influential leader of the Republican party of our State. The truth is, you were, fortunately, placed in such a position that you were enabled to render a great service to a Mississippi Democrat without doing a single act, or giving expression to a single thought, that was not in harmony with your position as a leader of your own party. That you saw fit to make me, rather than some other Democrat, the beneficiary of your partiality is what I keenly appreciate, highly value and now desire to reciprocate. The Republican party is now out of power, and it is likely to remain so for the next quarter of a century. Fortunately for me I am now so situated that I can reciprocate, in a small measure, the friendly interest you have taken in me in the recent past; and this, I hope, you will allow me to do. I have an office at my disposal that I want you to accept. I know you are a pronounced

Republican.   I neither ask nor expect you to change your politics.   Knowing you as I do, it would be useless for me to make such a request of you even if I desired to have you make such a change.   All I shall ask of you is that you be not offensively active or boldly aggressive in political matters while you hold a commission from me.   In other words, I want to render you a service without having you compromise your political standing, and without making the slightest change in your party affiliations. However, recognizing as you must the delicacy of the situation resulting from the position I occupy and the relation that I sustain to the administration, you will, I know, refrain from saying and doing anything that will place me in an embarrassing position before the public and before the administration with which I am identified.   The office to which I refer is that of special agent of public lands. The salary is fifteen hundred a year and expenses. The place is worth from two thousand to two thousand five hundred a year.   I shall not send you down South, where you may have some unpleasant and embarrassing experiences, but I will send you out into the Black Hills, where you will not be subjected to the slightest inconvenience and where you will have very little to do, but make your reports and draw your pay.   If you say you will accept the apopintment I shall give immediate direc-

tions for the commission to be made out and you
can take the oath of office within the next twenty-
four hours."

Of course I listened with close attention and with
deep interest to what the honorable Secretary said.
When he had finished, I replied in about these
words:

" Mr. Secretary, I fully appreciate the friendly interest you manifest in me, and I also appreciate
what you are willing to do for me. If I have rendered you any services in the past, I can assure you
that they were not rendered with the expectation
that you would thereby be placed under any obligations to me whatever. If I preferred you to others
in your own party it was because I believed in you
the State would have the services of one of its best,
most brilliant and most eloquent representatives.
It was the good of the State and the best interests
of its people rather than the personal advancement
of an individual that actuated me. The exalted
position now occupied by you I consider a confirmation of the wisdom of my decision. But the fact
cannot be overlooked that while you are an able and
influential leader in the Democratic party, I am,
though not so able nor so influential, a leader,—
locally, if not nationally,— in the Republican party.
While I can neither hope nor expect to reach that
point of honor and distinction in the Republican
party that you have reached in the Democratic, I

am just as proud of the position I occupy to-day as a Republican, as it is possible for you to be of yours as a Democrat.   Even if it be true, as you predict — of course I do not agree with you — that the Republican party will be out of power for the next quarter of a century, or even if that party should never again come into power, that fact cannot and will not have the slightest weight with me.   Therefore, I do not feel that you, as a member of a National Democratic Administration, can afford to tender me any position that I can see my way clear to accept.   While I fully and keenly appreciate your friendly interest in me and your desire and willingness to serve me, I cannot accept the position you have so gracefully tendered me, nor can I accept any other you may see fit to offer me.

" But, if you want to render me a service, I can tell you wherein it can be done,— a service that will be just as much appreciated as any you can possibly render me.   When I was a member of Congress I secured the appointment of quite a number of young colored men to clerkships in the Pension Bureau of your department.   I understand that all these men have excellent records.   If you will retain them in their positions I shall feel that you have repaid me for whatever you may think I have done for you in the past."

" That," the Secretary replied, " is a very reasonable request.   Come to see me again in a day or two and bring a list of their names and I will then see just what I can do along those lines."

I then bade Mr. Lamar good-bye and left his office. A few days later I returned with the list. But upon that list I had placed the names of two men who had not been appointed on my recommendation. One was a colored man, a physician; the other was a white man, a lawyer. The physician occupied a position that was in the line of his profession. The lawyer was a clerk in the Pension Bureau, who had been recently appointed upon the recommendation of Senator Bruce. The physician had been connected with the public service a long time. I knew both men favorably and felt that it was my duty to save them if in my power. Both were married and had interesting families.

When I placed the list in the Secretary's hands he read it over very carefully, and then said:

" I think I can safely assure you that the name of every one on this list will be retained except these two "— indicating the colored physician and the white lawyer. " This physician," the Secretary said, " is a colored man, and the husband of a white wife. The lawyer is a white man, and the husband of a colored wife. I cannot promise you, therefore, that they will be retained, however capable and efficient they may be. So far as I am personally concerned, it would make no material difference; I should just as lief retain them as any of the others.   But I cannot afford to antagonize public opinion in my State on the question of amalgamation.   One of these men, the white lawyer, is from my own State, where he is well known.   His case is recent, and fresh in the public mind.   So far as he is concerned, I can see no escape.   With the colored physician it may be different.   He is not from my State and is not known in the State.   I doubt very much if anyone in the State knows anything about him, or is aware of the fact that the position occupied by him is under my department.   If attention is not called to his case, I shall let him alone.

"But with the lawyer it is different.   A representative of a Mississippi newspaper that is unfriendly to me is now on the ground.   He has a list of all the Republicans,— especially the colored ones,— holding positions in this department.   The name of this lawyer is on that list.   It is the intention of the faction his paper represents to bring pressure to bear upon me to force me to turn all of these men out of office for political reasons, regardless of their official standing.   But, so far as your friends are concerned, I shall defy them except in the case of this lawyer, and also in the case of this physician if attention is called to him.   In their cases, or either of them, I shall be obliged, for reasons already given; to yield."

Strange to say, attention was never called to the

case of the physician and he remained in office during the whole of Mr. Cleveland's first administration. I made a strong appeal to the Secretary in
behalf of my friend, the white lawyer. I said in
substance:

"Mr. Secretary, you ought not to allow this de-
serving man to be punished simply because he was
brave enough to legally marry the woman of his
choice. You know him personally. You know him
to be an able and brilliant young man. You know
that he is now discharging the responsible duties of
the position which he occupies in your department
with credit to himself, and to the satisfaction of his
official superiors. You know that you have not a
better nor a more capable official connected with the
public service than you have in this able young man.
Under these circumstances it is your duty, as the
responsible head of your department, to protect him
and his estimable family from this gross wrong,—
this cruel injustice. For no one knows better than
you do, Mr. Secretary, that this alleged opposition
to amalgamation is both hypocritical and insincere.
If a natural antipathy existed between the two races
no law would be necessary to keep them apart.
The law, then, against race intermarriage has a
tendency to encourage and promote race intermixture, rather than to discourage and prevent it; because under existing circumstances local sentiment
in our part of the country tolerates the intermix-

ture, provided that the white husband and father does not lead to the altar in honorable wedlock the woman he may have selected as the companion of his life, and the mother of his children. If, instead of prohibiting race intermarriage, the law would compel marriage in all cases of concubinage, such a law would have a tendency to discourage race intermixture; because it is only when they marry according to the forms of law that the white husband and father is socially and otherwise ostracized. Under the common law,— which is the established and recognized rule of action in all of our States in the absence of a local statute by which a different rule is established,— a valid marriage is nothing more than a civil contract entered into between two persons capable of making contracts. But under our form of government marriage, like everything else, is what public opinion sees fit to make it.

"It is true that in our part of the country no union of the sexes is looked upon as a legal marriage unless the parties to the union are married according to the form prescribed by the local statutes. While that is true it is also true that there are many unions, which, but for the local statutes, would be recognized and accepted as legal marriages and which, even under existing conditions, are tolerated by local sentiment and sanctioned by custom. Such unions are known to exist, and yet are presumed not to exist. None are so blind as those who can see but will not see. One of the unwritten but most effective and rigid laws of our section,— which everyone respects and never violates,— is that a man's private and domestic life must never be made the subject of political or public discussion or newspaper notoriety. The man, who at any time or under any provocation will so far forget himself as to say or do anything that can be construed into a violation of that unwritten law, will be likely to pay the penalty with his own life and that, too, without court, judge, or jury; and the one by whom the penalty may be inflicted will stand acquitted and justified before the bar of public opinion. If, then, this able and brilliant young man,— whose bread and meat you now have at your disposal, —had lived in concubinage with the mother of his children, no law against custom and tradition would have been violated, and no one would suggest that he be punished for what he had done. Knowing these facts as you do, you ought to rise to the dignity of the occasion and protect this good and innocent man from the cruel, unjust, and unreasonable demands that are now being made upon you to dispense with his valuable services. This gentleman, to my personal knowledge, is not only worthy of whatever you may do for him, but his elegant and accomplished wife is one of the finest and most cultivated ladies it has ever been my good fortune to know. She is not only remarkably intelligent, but she is a woman of fine natural ability and of superior attainments. She is such a brilliant conversationalist,— so interesting, so instructive and so entertaining,— that it is a great pleasure and satisfaction to have the opportunity of being in her delightful presence, and of sitting within the sound of her sweet, charming, and musical voice. In physical development she is as near perfection as it is possible for a woman to be. I have had the good fortune of knowing her well for a number of years, and I have always admired her for her excellent traits and admirable qualities. She is a woman that would ornament and grace the parlor and honor the home of the finest and best man that ever lived, regardless of his race or nationality or the station he may occupy in life, however exalted that station may be. She married the man of her choice because she had learned to love and honor him, and because, in her opinion, he possessed everything, except wealth, that was calculated to contribute to her comfort, pleasure and happiness. In a recent conversation I had with her, her beautiful, large dark eyes sparkled with delight, and her sweet and lovely face was suffused with a smile of satisfaction when she informed me that she had never had occasion to regret her selection of a husband. She was then the mother of several very handsome children, to whom she pointed with pardonable pride. The products of such a union could not possibly be otherwise than attractive, for the father was a remarkably handsome man, while the mother was a personification of the typical southern beauty. The man was devoted to his family. How could he be otherwise? Husband and wife were so strongly attached to each other that both were more than willing to make any sacrifice that cruel fate might have in store for them.

"I therefore appeal to you, Mr. Secretary, in behalf of this charming and accomplished woman and her sweet and lovely children. In taking this position I am satisfied you will have nothing to lose, for you will not only have right on your side, but the interest of the public service as well. Rise, then, to the dignity of the occasion and assert and maintain your manhood and your independence. You have done this on previous occasions, why not do it again? As a member of the Senate of the United States you openly and publicly defied the well-known public sentiment of your party in the State which you then had the honor in part to represent, when you disregarded and repudiated the mandate of the State Legislature, instructing you to vote for the free and unlimited coinage of silver. It was that vote and the spirit of manly independence shown by you on that occasion that placed you in the high and responsible position you now occupy, the duties of which your friends know will be discharged in a way that will reflect credit upon yourself and honor upon your State.

" You again antagonized the dominant sentiment of the Democratic party of your State when you pronounced an eloquent eulogy upon the life and character of Charles Sumner. And yet you were able to overcome the bitter opposition you had encountered on each of those occasions. You can do the same thing in this case. I therefore ask you to promise me that this worthy and competent public servant shall not be discharged as long as his official record remains good."

The Secretary listened to my remarks with close and respectful attention. When I had finished he said:

" I agree with nearly all you have said. My sympathies are with your friend and it is my desire to retain him in the position he now so satisfactorily fills. But when you ask me to disregard and openly defy the well-known sentiment of the white people of my State on the question of amalgamation, I fear you make a request of me which I cannot safely grant, however anxious I may be to serve you. I could defend myself before a public audience in my State on the silver question and on the Sumner eulogy much more successfully than on the question of amalgamation; although in the main, I recognize the force and admit the truth of what you have said upon that subject. Hypocritical and insincere as the claim may be with reference to maintaining the absolute separation of the two races, the sentiment on that subject is one which no man who is ambitious to have a political future can safely afford to ignore,— especially under the new order of things about which you are well posted. While I am sorry for your friend, and should be pleased to grant your request in his case, I cannot bring myself to a realization of the fact that it is one of sufficient national importance to justify me in taking the stand you have so forcibly and eloquently suggested."

This ended the interview. I went to the home of my friend that evening, and informed him and his amiable wife of what had been said and done. They thanked me warmly for my efforts in their behalf, and assured me that there was a future before them, and that in the battle of life they were determined to know no such word as " fail." A few weeks later my friend's official connection with the public service was suddenly terminated. He and his family then left Washington for Kansas, I think. About a year thereafter he had occasion to visit Washington on business. I happened to be there at that time. He called to see me and informed me that, instead of regretting what had occurred, he had every reason to be thankful for it, since he had done very much better than he could have done had he remained at Washington. I was, of course, very much gratified to hear this and warmly congratulated him. Since that time, however, I have not seen him nor any member of his family, nor have I heard anything from them except indirectly, although I have made a number of unsuccessful efforts to find them. I am inclined to the opinion that, like thousands of people of the same class, their indentity with the colored race has long since ceased and that they have been absorbed by the white race, as I firmly believe will be true of the great mass of colored Americans. It is to prevent any embarrassment growing out of the probability of this condition that has actuated me in not making public the names of the parties in question. No good could come of the disclosure, and much harm might follow. I can, however, most positively assure the public that this is not a fiction,— that it is not a mere picture that is painted from the vividness of my imagination, but that the story as related in all its details is based upon actual occurrences.

With this one exception, Secretary Lamar retained in office every clerk whose name appeared on the list that I gave him. They were not only retained throughout the Administration but many of them were promoted. It can be said to the credit of Secretary Lamar that during his administration very few changes were made in the clerical force of the department for political reasons, and, as a rule, the clerks were treated with justice, fairness and impartiality.

CHAPTER XXV

THE FEDERAL ELECTIONS BILL

It was during the administration of President Harrison that another effort was made to secure the enactment by Congress of the necessary legislation for the effective enforcement of the war amendments to the National Constitution,— a Federal Elections Bill. Mr. Lodge, of Massachusetts, was the author of the bill. But the fact was soon developed that there were so many Republicans in and out of Congress who lacked the courage of their convictions that it would be impossible to secure favorable action. In fact there were three classes of white men at the South who claimed to be Republicans who used their influence to defeat that contemplated legislation. The white men at the South who acted with the Republican party at that time were divided into four classes.

First, those who were Republicans from principle and conviction — because they were firm believers in the principles, doctrines, and policies for which the party stood, and were willing to remain with it in adversity as well as in prosperity,— in defeat as well as in victory. This class, I am pleased to say, while not the most noisy and demonstrative, comprised over seventy-five per cent. of the white membership of the party in that part of the country.

Second, a small but noisy and demonstrative group, comprising about fifteen per cent of the remainder, who labored under the honest, but erroneous, impression that the best and most effective way to build up a strong Republican party at the South was to draw the color line in the party. In other words, to organize a Republican party to be composed exclusively of white men, to the entire exclusion of colored men. What those men chiefly wanted,— or felt the need of for themselves and their families,— was social recognition by the better element of the white people of their respective localities. They were eager, therefore, to bring about such a condition of things as would make it possible for them to be known as Republicans without subjecting themselves and their families to the risk of being socially ostracized by their white Democratic neighbors. And then again those men believed then, and some of them still believe or profess to believe, that southern Democrats were and are honest and sincere in the declaration that the presence of the colored men in the Republican party prevented southern white men from coming into it. " Draw the race line against the colored man,— organize a white Republican party,— and

you will find that thousands of white men who
now act with the Democratic party will join the
Republicans." Some white Republicans believed
that the men by whom these declarations were made
were honest and sincere,— and it may be that some
of them were,— but it appears not to have occurred
to them that if the votes of the colored men were
suppressed the minority white vote, unaided and
unprotected, would be powerless to prevent the application of methods which would nullify any
organized effort on their part. In other words,
nothing short of an effective national law, to protect the weak against the strong and the minority
of the whites against the aggressive assaults of the
majority of that race, would enable the minority of
the whites to make their power and influence effective and potential; and even then it could be ef-
fectively done only in coöperation with the blacks.
Then again, they seemed to have lost sight of the
fact,— or perhaps they did not know it to be a
fact,— that many leading southern Democrats are
insincere in their declarations upon the so-called
race question. They keep that question before the
public for political and party reasons only, because
they find it to be the most effective weapon they
can use to hold the white men in political subjection. The effort, therefore, to build up a " white "
Republican party at the South has had a tendency,
under existing circumstances, to discourage a

strong Republican organization in that section. But, even if it were possible for such an organization to have a potential existence, it could not be otherwise than ephemeral, because it would be wholly out of harmony with the fundamental principles and doctrines of the national organization whose name it had appropriated. It would be in point of fact a misnomer and, therefore, wholly out of place as one of the branches of the national organization which stands for, defends, and advocates the civil and political equality of all American citizens, without regard to race, color, nationality, or religion. Any organization, therefore, claiming to be a branch of the Republican party, but which had repudiated and denounced the fundamental and sacred creed of that organization, would be looked upon by the public as a close, selfish and local machine that was brought into existence to serve the ends, and satisfy the selfish ambition of the promoters and organizers of the corporation. Yet there were a few well-meaning and honest white men in some of the Southern States who were disposed, through a mistaken sense of political necessity, to give such a movement the benefit of their countenance. But the movement has been a lamentable failure in States where it has been tried, and it cannot be otherwise in States where it may yet be tried. Men who were in sympathy with a movement of this sort took a pronounced stand against the proposed Federal Elections Bill, and used what influence they had to prevent its passage; their idea being that, if passed, it would have a tendency to prevent the accomplishment of the purposes they had in contemplation.

Third, a group that consisted of a still smaller number who were Republicans for revenue only,— for the purpose of getting office. If an office were in sight they would be quite demonstrative in their advocacy of the Republican party and its principles; but if they were not officially recognized, their activities would not only cease, but they would soon be back into the fold of the Democracy. But should they be officially recognized they would be good, faithful, and loyal Republicans,— at least so far as words were concerned,— until they ceased to be officials, when they would cease at the same time to be Republicans. Men of this class were, of course, opposed to the proposed legislation for the enforcement of the war amendments to the Constitution.

Fourth, a group that consisted of an insignificantly small number of white men who claimed to be national Republicans and local Democrats,— that is, they claimed that they voted for the Republican candidate for President every four years, but for Democrats in all other elections. Of course they were against the proposed legislation. These men succeeded in inducing some well-meaning Republican members of Congress, like Senator Washburne, of Minnesota, for instance, to believe that the passage of such a bill would have a tendency to prevent the building up of a strong Republican organization at the South. Then again, the free silver question was before the public at that time. The Republican majority in the Senate was not large. Several of those who had been elected as Republicans were free silver men. On that question they were in harmony with a majority of the Democrats, and out of harmony with the great majority of Republicans. The Free Silver Republicans, therefore, were not inclined to support a measure that was particularly offensive to their friends and allies on the silver question. After a careful canvass of the Senate it was developed that the Republican leaders could not safely count on the support of any one of the Free Silver Republicans in their efforts to pass the bill, and, since they had the balance of power, any further effort to pass it was abandoned. It was then made plain to the friends and supporters of that measure that no further attempt would be made in that direction for a long time, if ever.

I wrote and had published in the Washington *Post* a letter in which I took strong grounds in favor of having the representation in Congress,— from States where the colored men had been practically disfranchised through an evasion of the Fifteenth Amendment,— reduced in the manner prescribed by the Fourteenth Amendment. In that letter I made an effort to answer every argument that had been made in opposition to such a proposition. It had been argued by some fairly good lawyers, for instance, that the subsequent ratification of the Fifteenth Amendment had so modified the Fourteenth as to take away from Congress this optional and discretionary power which had been previously conferred upon it by the Fourteenth Amendment. I tried in that letter,— and I think I succeeded,— to answer the argument on that point. It was also said that if Congress were to take such a step it would thereby give its sanction to the disfranchisement of the colored men in the States where that had been done. This I think I succeeded in proving was untrue and without foundation. The truth is that the only material difference between the Fourteenth and Fifteenth Amendments on this particular point is that, subsequent to the ratification of the Fourteenth and prior to the ratification of the Fifteenth Amendment, a State could legally disfranchise white or colored men on account of race or color, but, since the ratification of the Fifteenth Amendment, this cannot be legally done. If, then, Congress had the constitutional right under the Fourteenth Amendment to punish a State in the manner therein prescribed, for doing what the State then had a legal and constitutional right to do, I cannot see why Congress has not now the same power and authority to inflict the same punishment upon the State for doing or permitting to be done what it now has no legal and constitutional right to do.

No State, in my opinion, should be allowed to take advantage of its own wrongs, and thus, by a wrongful act, augment its own power and influence in the government. To allow a majority of the white men in the State of Mississippi, for instance, to appropriate to themselves through questionable methods the representative strength of the colored population of that State, excluding the latter from all participation in the selection of the representatives in Congress, is a monstrous wrong, the continuance of which should not be tolerated.

For every crime there must be a punishment; for every wrong there must be a remedy, and for every grievance there must be a redress. That this state of things is wrong and unjust, if not unlawful, no fair-minded person will deny. It is not only wrong and unjust to the colored people of the State, who are thus denied a voice in the government under which they live and to support which they are taxed, but it also involves a grave injustice to the States in which the laws are obeyed and the National Constitution,— including the war amendments to the same,— is respected and enforced. I am aware of the fact that it is claimed by those who are responsible for what is here complained of that, while the acts referred to may be an evasion if not a violation of the *spirit* of the Constitution, yet, since they do not violate the *letter* of the Constitution the complaining parties are without a remedy, and therefore have no redress.   This contention is not only weak in logic but unsound in law, even as construed by the Supreme Court of the United States, which tribunal seems to be the last to which an appeal can be successfully made, having for its object the enforcement of the Constitution and laws so far as they relate to the political and civil rights of the colored Americans.   That a State can do by indirection what it cannot do directly, is denied even by the Supreme Court of the United States.

That doctrine was clearly and distinctly set forth in a decision of the Court rendered by Mr. Justice Strong, which was concurred in by a majority of his associates.   In that decision it was held that affirmative State action is not necessary to constitute race discrimination by the State.   In other words, in order to constitute affirmative State action in violation of the Constitutional mandate against distinction and discrimination based on race or color, it is not necessary that the State should pass a law for that purpose.   The State, the Court declared, acts through its agents, Legislative, Executive and Judicial.   Whenever an agent or representative of the State acts, his acts are binding upon the State, and the effect is the same as if the State had passed a law for that purpose. If a judge, for example, in the selection of jurors to serve in his court should knowingly and intentionally allow a particular race to be excluded from such service on account of race or color, the effect would be the same as if the State, through its Legislature, had passed a law for that purpose. The colored men in the States complained of, have been disfranchised in violation of the spirit if not the letter of the Constitution, either by affirmative State action, or through and by the State's agents and representatives. Their acts, therefore, constitute State action as fully as if the Legislature had passed a law for that purpose.

CHAPTER XXVI

MISSISSIPPI AND THE NULLIFICATION OF THE FIFTEENTH AMENDMENT

The defeat or abandonment of the Lodge Federal Elections Bill was equivalent to a declaration that no further attempts would be made for a good while, at least, to enforce by appropriate legislation the war amendments to the Constitution. Southern Democrats were not slow in taking advantage of the knowledge of that fact.

My own State, Mississippi, was the first to give legal effect to the practical nullification of the Fifteenth Amendment. On that question the Democratic party in the State was divided into two factions. The radical faction, under the leadership of Senator George, advocated the adoption and enforcement of extreme methods. The liberal or conservative faction,— or what was known as the Lamar wing of the party under the leadership of Senator Walthall,— was strongly opposed to such methods. Senator George advocated the calling of a Constitutional Convention, to frame a new Constitution for the State. Senator Walthall opposed it, contending that the then Constitution,

though framed by Republicans, was, in the main.
unobjectionable and should be allowed to stand.
But Senator George was successful, and a convention was called to meet in the fall of 1890. In
order to take no chances the Senator had himself
nominated and elected a member of the Convention.

When the Convention met, it was found that
there were two strong factions, one in favor of giving legal effect to the nullification of the Fifteenth
Amendment, and the other opposed to it. The
George faction was slightly in the majority, resulting in one of their number,— nullificationists,
as they were called,— Judge S. S. Calhoun, being
elected President of the Convention. The plan advocated and supported by the George faction, of
which Senator George was the author, provided
that no one be allowed to register as a voter, or vote
if registered, unless he could read and write, or
unless he could understand any section of the Constitution when read to him and give a reasonable interpretation thereof. This was known as the
"understanding clause." It was plain to every
one that its purpose was to evade the Fifteenth
Amendment, and disfranchise the illiterate voters
of one race without disfranchising those of the
other.

The opposition to this scheme was under the leadership of one of the ablest and most brilliant members of the bar, Judge J. B. Christman, of Lincoln

County.   As a substitute for the George plan or understanding clause, he ably and eloquently advocated the adoption of a fair and honest educational qualification as a condition precedent to registration and voting, to be equally applicable to whites and blacks.

The speeches on both sides were able and interesting.   It looked for a while as if the substitute clause proposed by Judge Christman would be adopted.   In consequence of such an apprehension, Judge Calhoun, the President of the Convention, took the floor in opposition to the Christman plan, and in support of the one proposed by Senator George.   The substance of his speech was that the Convention had been called for the purpose of insuring the ascendency of the white race,— the Democratic party,— in the administration of the State Government through some other methods than those which had been enforced since 1875.

" If you fail in the discharge of your duties in this matter," he declared, " the blood of every negro that will be killed in an election riot hereafter will be upon your shoulders."

In other words, the speaker frankly admitted, what everyone knew to be a fact, that the ascendency of the Democratic party in the State had been maintained since 1875 through methods which, in his opinion, should no longer be sanctioned and tolerated.   These methods, he contended, were corrupting the morals of the people of the State and should be discontinued; but the ascendency of the Democratic party must be maintained at any cost. The George plan, he urged, would accomplish this result, because if the negroes were disfranchised according to the forms of law, there would be no occasion to suppress his vote by violence because he would have no vote to suppress; and there would be no occasion to commit fraud in the count or perjury in the returns.

Notwithstanding this frank speech, which was intended to arouse the fears of the members of the Convention from a party standpoint, the defeat of the Christman substitute was by no means an assured fact. But the advocates of the George plan,— the " understanding clause,"— were both desperate and determined. Contrary to public expectation two Republicans, Geo. B. Melchoir and I. T. Montgomery, had been elected to the Convention from Bolivar County. But their seats were contested, and it was assumed that their Democratic contestants would be seated. Still, pending the final disposition of the case, the two Republicans were the sitting members. Montgomery was colored and Melchoir was white. But the George faction needed those two votes. No one suspected, however, that they would get them in any other way than by seating the contestants. The advocates and supporters of the Christman substitute were, therefore, very much surprised and disappointed when they learned that Mr. Montgomery, the only colored member of the Convention, intended to make a speech in favor of the adoption of the George plan, and vote for it; which he did.   Why this man, who had the reputation of being honest and honorable, and who in point of intelligence was considerably above the average of his race, should have thus acted and voted has always been an inexplicable mystery.   It is difficult to believe that he was willing to pay such a price for the retention of his seat in the Convention, still it is a fact that the contest was never called and Montgomery and his colleague were allowed to retain their seats.

The adoption of the George plan was thus assured, but not without a desperate fight.   The opponents of that scheme made a brave, though unsuccessful, fight against it.   But it was soon made plain to the advocates of the George plan that what they had succeeded in forcing through the Convention would be defeated by the people at the ballot-box.   In fact, a storm of protest was raised throughout the State.   The Democratic press, as well as the members of that party, were believed to be about equally divided on the question of the ratification of the Constitution as thus framed.   Since it was well known that the Republicans would be solid in their opposition to ratification, the rejection of the proposed Constitution was an assured fact.   But the supporters of the George scheme felt that they could not afford to have the results of their labors go down in defeat. In order to prevent this they decided to deny the people the right of passing judgment upon the work of the Convention. The decision, therefore, was that the Convention by which the Constitution was framed should declare it duly ratified and approved, and to go into effect upon a day therein named. The people of that unfortunate State, therefore, have never had an opportunity to pass judgment upon the Constitution under which they are living and which they are required to obey and support, that right having been denied them because it was known that a majority of them were opposed to its ratification and would have voted against it.

But this so-called "understanding clause," or George scheme, is much more sweeping than was intended by its author. The intent of that clause was to make it possible to disfranchise the illiterate blacks without disfranchising the illiterate whites. But as construed and enforced it is not confined to illiterates but to persons of intelligence as well. No man, for instance, however intelligent he may be, can be registered as a voter or vote if registered, if the registering officers or the election officers are of the opinion that he does not understand the Constitution. It is true, the instrument is so worded that no allusion is made to the

race or color of those seeking to be registered and
to vote; still, it is perfectly plain to everyone that
the purpose was to enable the State to do, through
its authorized and duly appointed agents and representatives, the very thing the Fifteenth Amendment declares shall not be done.   According to the
decision of the Supreme Court, as rendered by Mr.
Justice Strong, the effect is the same as if the instrument had declared in so many words that race or
color should be the basis of discrimination and exclusion.

The bitter and desperate struggle between the
two factions of the Democratic party in the State
of Mississippi in this contest, forcibly illustrates
the fact that the National Republican party made a
grave mistake when it abandoned any further effort to enforce by appropriate legislation the war
amendments to the Constitution.   In opposing and
denouncing the questionable methods of the extreme and radical faction of their own party, the
conservative faction of the Democrats believed, expected, and predicted that such methods would not
be acquiesced in by the Republican party, nor would
they be tolerated by the National Government.   If
those expectations and predictions had been verified they would have given the conservative element
a justifiable excuse to break away from the radicals,
and this would have resulted in having two strong
political parties in that section to-day instead of

one. But when it was seen that the National Republican party made no further opposition to the enforcement of those extraneous, radical and questionable methods, that fact not only had the effect of preventing further opposition on the part of the conservative Democrats, but it also resulted in many of the politically ambitious among them joining the ranks of the radicals, since that was then the only channel through which it was possible for their political aspirations to be gratified.

The reader cannot fail to see that under the plan in force in Mississippi there is no incentive to intelligence; because intelligence does not secure access to the ballot-box, nor does the lack of it prevent such access. It is not an incentive to the accumulation of wealth; because the ownership of property does not secure to the owner access to the ballot-box, nor does the lack of it prevent such access. It is not a question of intelligence, wealth or character, nor can it be said that it is wholly a question of party. It is simply a question of factional affiliation. The standard of qualification is confined to such white men as may be in harmony with the faction that may happen to have control for the time being of the election machinery. What is true of Mississippi in this respect is equally true of the other States in which schemes of various sorts have been invented and adopted to evade the Fifteenth Amendment to the Constitution.

CHAPTER XXVII

EFFECT OF THE MCKINLEY TARIFF BILL ON BOTH
POLITICAL PARTIES

The Congressional elections of 1890 resulted in a crushing defeat for the Republicans. This was due, no doubt, to the McKinley Tariff Bill which became a law only about a month before the elections of that year. Congress convened the first Monday in December, 1889, and that session did not come to a close until the following October. The Democrats in Congress made a bitter fight against the McKinley Tariff Bill, and, since it was a very complete and comprehensive measure, a great deal of time was necessarily consumed in its consideration and discussion. When it finally became a law the time between its passage and the elections was so short that the friends of the measure did not have time to explain and defend it before the elections took place. This placed the Republicans at a great disadvantage. They were on the defensive from the beginning. The result was a sweeping Democratic victory.

But, strange to say, the same issues that produced Democratic success and Republican defeat at that election brought about Republican success and Democratic defeat at the Presidential and Congressional elections in 1896. The McKinley Tariff Bill of 1890 was so popular six years later, that the author of that measure was deemed the strongest and most available man to place at the head of the Republican ticket as the candidate of that party for President. His election was a complete vindication of the wisdom of the measure of which he was the author and champion. In 1890 his bill was so unpopular that it resulted in his own defeat for reëlection to Congress. But this did not cause him to lose faith in the wisdom and the ultimate popularity of the bill which he was proud to have bear his name.

"A little time," said McKinley, "will prove the wisdom of the measure." In this he was not mistaken. His defeat for reëlection to Congress ultimately made him President of the United States; for the following year the Republicans of his State elected him Governor, which was a stepping-stone to the Presidency. All that was needed was an opportunity for the merits of his bill to be thoroughly tested. Shortly after its passage, but before it could be enforced or even explained, the people were led to believe that it was a harsh, cruel, and unjust measure, imposing heavy, unreasonable, and unnecessary taxes upon them, increasing the prices of the necessaries of life without a corresponding increase in the price of labor.   The people were in an ugly mood in anticipation of what was never fully realized.

It is true that the tariff was not the sole issue that resulted in such a sweeping Republican victory in the National elections of 1896.   The financial issue, which was prominent before the people at that time, was one of the contributory causes of that result.   Still it cannot be denied that McKinley's connection with the Tariff Bill of 1890 was what gave him the necessary national prominence to make him the most available man to be placed at the head of his party ticket for the Presidency that year.

CHAPTER XXVIII

INTERVIEW BETWEEN THE AUTHOR AND PRESIDENT
CLEVELAND AND SECRETARY GRESHAM

When Mr. Cleveland was inaugurated in 1893, I was Auditor of the Treasury for the Navy Department. Hon. J. G. Carlisle, of Kentucky, had been made Secretary of the Treasury. My resignation had been tendered, the acceptance of which I expected to see announced any day, but the change did not take place until August of that year.

While seated at my desk one day a messenger from the White House made his appearance, and I was informed that the President desired to see me in person. When I arrived at the White House I was immediately ushered into the President's private office, where he was seated alone at a desk engaged in reading a book or a magazine. It was at an hour when he was not usually accessible to the public. He received me in a very cordial way. He informed me that there was an important matter about which he desired to talk with me — to get the benefit of my opinion and experience. He assured me of his friendly interest in the colored people. It was his determination that they should have suitable and appropriate recognition under his administration. He said he was very much opposed to the color line in politics. There was no more reason why a man should be opposed or discriminated against on account of his race than on account of his religion. He believed it to be the duty of the Democratic party to encourage the colored voters to divide their votes, and the best way to do this was to accord to that race the same relative consideration, the same treatment, and to give the race the same recognition that is given other races and classes of which our citizenship is composed. The party line is the only one that should be drawn. He would not appoint a colored Republican to office merely for the purpose of giving official recognition to the colored race, nor would he refuse to appoint a colored Democrat simply because he was colored. If this course were pursued, and this policy adopted and adhered to by the Democratic party, the colored voters who are in harmony with that party on questions about which white men usually divide, could see their way clear to vote in accordance with their convictions upon such issues, and would not be obliged to vote against the party with which they may be in harmony on account of that party's attitude towards them as a race. " In other words," he said, " it is a well-known fact that there are thousands of colored men who vote the Republican ticket at many important elections,— not from choice but from what they believe to be a necessity. If the views entertained by me on this subject should be accepted by the Democratic party, as I hope and believe they will be, that necessity,— real or imaginary,— would no longer exist, and the gradual division of the colored vote would necessarily follow."

He went on to say that he had not hesitated to express himself fully, freely and frankly with members of his own party on the subject, and that he had informed them of the course he intended to pursue; but that he had been advised against appointing any colored man to an office in which white women were employed.

"Now," said the President, "since you have been at the head of an important bureau in the Treasury Department during the past four years, a bureau in which a number of white women are employed as clerks, I desire very much to know what has been your experiences along those lines." I informed the President that I would take pleasure in giving him the information desired. I assured him that if my occupancy of that office had been the occasion of the slightest embarrassment to anyone connected with the public service,— whether in the office over which I presided or any other,— that fact had never been brought to my notice. On the contrary, I had every reason to believe that no one who had previously occupied the position enjoyed the respect, good-will and friendship of the clerks and other employees to a greater extent than was enjoyed by me. My occupancy of that office had more than demonstrated the fact, if such were necessary, that official position and social contact were separate and distinct. My contact with the clerks and other employees of the office was official, not social. During office hours they were subject to my direction and supervision in the discharge of their official duties, and I am pleased to say that all of them, without a single exception, have shown me that courtesy, deference and respect due to the head of the office. After office hours they went their way and I went mine. No new social ties were created and none were broken or changed as the result of the official position occupied by me. I assured the President, that, judging from my own experience, he need not have the slightest apprehension of any embarrassment, friction or unpleasantness growing out of the appointment of a colored man of intelligence, good judgment and wise discretion as head of any bureau in which white women were employed.

I could not allow the interview to close without expressing to the President my warm appreciation of his fair, just, reasonable and dignified position on the so-called race question.

" Your attitude," I said, " if accepted in good faith by your party, will prove to be the solution of this mythical race problem. Although I am a pronounced Republican, yet, as a colored American, I am anxious to have such a condition of things brought about as will allow a colored man to be a Democrat if he so desires. I believe you have stated the case accurately when you say that thousands of colored men have voted the Republican ticket at important elections, from necessity and not from choice. As a Republican, it is my hope that colored as well as white men, act with and vote for the candidates of that party when worthy and meritorious, but as a colored American, I want them to be so situated that they can vote that way from choice and not from necessity. No man can be a free and independent American citizen who is obliged to sacrifice his convictions upon the altar of his personal safety. The attitude of the Democratic party upon this so-called race question has made the colored voter a dependent, and not an independent, American citizen. The Republican party emancipated him from physical bondage, for which he is grateful. It remains for the Democratic party to emancipate him from political bondage, for which he will be equally grateful. You are engaged, Mr. President, in a good and glorious work. As a colored man I thank you for the brave and noble stand you have taken. God grant that you, as a Democrat, may have influence enough to get the Democratic party as an organization to support you in the noble stand you have so bravely taken."

The President thanked me for my expressions of good-will, and thus terminated what to me was a remarkable as well as a pleasant and most agreeable interview.

A few days later a messenger from the State Department called at my office and informed me that the Secretary of State, Judge Gresham, desired to see me. Judge Gresham and I had been warm personal friends for many years. He had occupied many positions of prominence and responsibility. He had been a major-general in the Union army, and was with Sherman's army during that celebrated March through Georgia. He was one of the leading candidates for the Presidential nomination before the National Republican Convention at Chicago in 1888, when General Benjamin Harrison, of Indiana, was nominated.

I was a member of that Convention and one of Judge Gresham's active supporters. In the campaign that followed Judge Gresham gave General Harrison his active and loyal support, but, for some unaccountable reason, he supported Mr. Cleveland against General Harrison in 1892. Mr. Cleveland was not only elected, but, contrary to public expectation, he carried the State of Illinois,— a State in which Judge Gresham was known to be very popular, especially among the colored people of

Chicago; many of whom, it was said, voted for Mr. Cleveland through the efforts and influence of Judge Gresham. Mr. Cleveland evidently believed that his success in Illinois was due largely to Judge Gresham, and as evidence of that fact, and because Judge Gresham was known to be a very able man, Mr. Cleveland paid him the distinguished honor of appointing him to the leading position in his cabinet,— that of Secretary of State.

When I called at the State Department the Judge invited me to a seat in his private office. He said there was an important matter about which he desired to talk with me. My name, he said, had been the subject of a recent conversation between the President and himself. The President, he said, was well aware of the cordial relations existing between us, and believed that if any man could influence my action he, Gresham, was that man.

"Now," said the Judge, "the President has formed a very favorable opinion of you. He is anxious to have you remain at the head of the important bureau over which you are now presiding in such a creditable and satisfactory manner. But you understand that it is a political office. As anxious as the President is to retain you, and as anxious as I am to have him do so, he could not do it and you could neither ask nor expect him to do it, unless you were known to be in sympathy with, and a supporter of, his administration,— at least in the main. Now, you know that I am not only your friend, but that I am a friend to the colored people. I know you are a Republican. So am I; but I am a Cleveland man. Cleveland is a better Republican than Harrison. In supporting Cleveland against Harrison I am no less a Republican. As your friend I would not advise you to do anything that would militate against your interests. Knowing, as you do, that I am not only your friend but also a good Republican, you can at least afford to follow where I lead. I want you, then, to authorize me to say to the President that you are in sympathy with the main purposes of his administration as explained to you by me, and that his decision to retain you in your present position will be fully and keenly appreciated by you."

In my reply I stated that while I was very grateful to the Judge for his friendly interest in me, and while I highly appreciated the President's good opinion of me, it would not be possible for me to consent to retain the position I then occupied upon the conditions named.

" If," I said, " it is the desire of the President to have me remain in charge of that office during his administration or any part thereof, I would be perfectly willing to do so if I should be permitted to remain free from any conditions, pledges, promises or obligations. The conditions suggested mean nothing more nor less than that I shall identify myself with the Democratic party. The President has no office at his disposal the acceptance or retention of which could be a sufficient inducement for me to take such a step as that. I agree with what you have said about Mr. Cleveland, so far as he is personally concerned. I have every reason to believe that he has a friendly interest in the colored people and that he means to do the fair thing by them so far as it may be in his power. But he was elected as a Democrat. He is the head of a National Democratic Administration. No man can be wholly independent of his party,— a fact recognized in the conditions suggested in my own case. I don't think that Mr. Cleveland is what would be called in my part of the country a good Democrat, because I believe he is utterly devoid of race prejudice, and is not in harmony with those who insist upon drawing the color line in the Democratic party. In my opinion he is in harmony with the Democratic party only on one important public question,— the tariff. On all others,— the so-called race question not excepted,— he is in harmony with what I believe to be genuine Republicanism. Still, as I have already stated, he was elected as a Democrat; and, since he holds that the office now occupied by me is a political one, it ought to be filled by one who is in political harmony with the administration. I am not that man; for I cannot truthfully say that

I am in harmony with the main purposes of the administration."

The Judge remarked that my decision was a disappointment to him, and he believed that I would some day regret having made it, but that he would communicate to the President the result of our interview. In spite of this, my successor, Morton, a Democrat from Maine, was not appointed until the following August.

CHAPTER XXIX

As a delegate to the National Republican Convention of 1900, I was honored by my delegation with being selected to represent Mississippi on the Committee on Platform and Resolutions; and by the chairman of that committee, Senator Fairbanks, I was made a member of the sub-committee that drafted the platform. At the first meeting of the sub-committee, the Ohio member, Senator J. B. Foraker, submitted the draft of a platform that had been prepared at Washington which was made the basis of quite a lengthy and interesting discussion. This discussion developed the fact that the Washington draft was not at all satisfactory to a majority of the sub-committee. The New York member, Hon. L. E. Quigg, was especially pronounced in his objections, not so much to what was declared, but to the manner and form in which the declarations were made. In his opinion, the principles of the party were not set forth in the Washington draft in language that would make them clearly understood and easily comprehended by the reading public. After every member who desired to speak had done so, it was agreed that those who desired amendments, changes, or additions should submit the same in writing, and that these with the Washington draft be turned over to Mr. Quigg as a sub-committee of one. A platform in harmony with the views expressed by members of the committee would then be carefully prepared, and the same submitted to the sub-committee at an adjourned meeting to be held at an early hour the next morning.

The only amendment suggested by me was one, the purpose of which was to express more clearly the attitude of the party with reference to the enforcement of the war amendments to the National Constitution. When the sub-committee met the next morning Mr. Quigg submitted an entirely new draft, which he had prepared the afternoon and night before, using the Washington draft and the amendments submitted by members of the sub-committee as the basis of what he had done. His draft proved to be so satisfactory to the sub-committee that it was accepted and adopted with very slight modifications. Mr. Quigg seemed to have been very careful in the preparation of his draft, not only giving expression to the views of the sub-committee, which had been developed in the discussion, and as had been set forth in the suggested amendments referred to him, but the manner and form of expression used by him impressed the committee as being a decided improvement upon the Washington draft, although the subject matter in both drafts was substantially the same. Mr. Quigg's draft, with very slight changes and alterations, was not only accepted and adopted, but he was the recipient of the thanks of the other members for the excellent manner in which he had discharged the important duty that had been assigned him.

The full committee was then convened by which the unanimous report of the sub-committee was adopted without opposition and without change. But I had anticipated a renewal of the effort to change the basis of representation in future National Republican Conventions, and had, therefore, made some little mental preparation to take a leading part in opposition to its adoption. Such a proposition had been submitted at nearly every National Convention of the party since 1884. That a similar effort would be made at this convention I had good reasons to believe. In this I was not mistaken. It was introduced by Senator Quay, of Pennsylvania. His proposition, like the others, was that in the future delegates to the National Convention should be apportioned among the different States upon the basis of the votes polled for the party candidates at the last preceding national election, instead of upon the basis of the States' representation in Congress. On the first view this proposition seems to be both reasonable and fair, but it cannot stand the

test of an intelligent analysis.   As soon as I sought
and secured the recognition of the chair, I offered
an amendment in the nature of a substitute, de-
claring it to be the judgment of the party that in all
States in which there had been an evasion of the
Fifteenth Amendment by State action, that there
should be a reduction in the representation in Congress from such State or States in the manner and
for the purpose expressed in the Fourteenth Amendment.   A point of order was immediately made
against the amendment, but the occupant of the
chair, Senator Lodge, stated that he would hold his
decision in reserve pending an explanation by me
of the amendment I had submitted.   At that time a
suggestion was made that the whole subject be
postponed until the next day, to which I assented,
and then yielded the floor.   But it was not again
called up, hence my speech was never delivered.
Since it may be of some interest to the reader to
get an idea of what I had in mind, I shall here set
down in the main what I intended to say on that
occasion had the opportunity been presented.

   " Mr. Chairman, while there may be some doubt,
in a parliamentary sense, as to whether or not the
amendment I have submitted can be entertained as
a substitute for the original proposition, it cannot
be denied that it relates to the same subject matter.
I hope, therefore, that the Convention will have an
opportunity in some way of voting upon it in lieu

of the one that has been presented by the distinguished gentleman from Pennsylvania. It is a well-known fact that under the present system each State is entitled to double the number of delegates that it has Senators and Representatives in Congress. The plan now proposed is that the apportionment in future conventions be based upon the number of votes polled for the candidates of the party at the last preceding National election, according to what is known as the ' official returns,' although it may be a fact, as is unquestionably true in some States, that the ' official returns ' may not be free from fraud,— that they may represent in some instances not the actual party vote polled, but the party vote counted, certified, and returned. This plan, therefore, means that representation from some States in future National Republican Conventions will not be based upon Republican strength, nor determined by Republican votes, but will be fixed and determined by Democratic election officials. In other words, Democrats, and not Republicans, will fix and determine in a large measure, representation in future Conventions of the Republican party.

" The proposed change is predicated upon the assumption that elections are fair and returns are honest in all the States at each and every National election. If that were true the difference in the representation from the several States would be unimportant and immaterial, even under the proposed change, hence there would be no occasion for the change.   The fact that this assumption is not true furnishes the basis for the alleged inequality in representation, and the apparent necessity for the change proposed.   In addition to this it is a well-known fact that in several of the Southern States, — my own, Mississippi, among the number,— the Fifteenth Amendment to the National Constitution has been practically nullified, and that the colored men in such States have been as effectually disfranchised as if the Fifteenth Amendment were not a part of the organic law of the land.   If the plan that is now proposed by the distinguished gentleman from Pennsylvania should be adopted, the National Republican party by accepting them and making them the basis of representation in future National Conventions of the party will have thereby placed itself on record as having given its sanction to the questionable methods by which these results have been accomplished.   I frankly confess that the plan I have presented is based upon the humiliating confession that the Government is without power under the Constitution as construed by the Supreme Court to effectually enforce the war amendments; and that in consequence thereof nothing is left to be done but to fall back upon the plan prescribed by the Fourteenth Amendment, which is to reduce the representation in Congress from such States in the manner and for the purposes therein stated.

"It is true that the Fourteenth Amendment having been proposed and submitted prior to the Fifteenth, the provision with reference to reduction of representation in Congress was predicated upon the assumption that the different States could then legally make race or color a ground of discrimination in prescribing the qualification of electors. Still, it occurs to me that if a State could be thus punished for doing that which it had a legal right to do, the same punishment can now be inflicted for doing that which it can no longer legally do. If the plan proposed by the distinguished gentleman from Pennsylvania should be adopted, the Republican party will not only have placed itself on record as having given its sanction to the methods by which these results will have been accomplished, but it will be notice to the different States, north as well as south, that any of them that may see fit to take advantage of their own wrongs will have no occasion to fear any future punishment being inflicted upon the State for so doing. Under the plan thus proposed the State that may thus take advantage of its own wrongs will not only receive no punishment in the reduction of its representation in Congress, but its methods and practices will have been approved and adopted by the Republican party.

"On the other hand, the plan I propose is one

which is equivalent to a notice to the different States that, while the National Government may not be able to enforce by appropriate legislation the war amendments to the Constitution, the Legislative department of the Government can prevent a State from taking advantage of its own wrongs, through the infliction of a punishment upon the State in the reduction of its representation in Congress. Since representation in the National Convention is based upon the States' representation in Congress, it will be seen that if the representation in Congress from such States should be reduced, it would result in a reduction in the representation from such States in the National Convention. The main purpose, therefore, which the distinguished gentleman from Pennsylvania seems to have in view will have been practically accomplished, but in a far different and in a much less objectionable way. It will be some satisfaction to southern Republicans, who are denied access to the ballot-box through an evasion of the National Constitution, to know that if they are to be denied a voice in future National Conventions of the party to which they belong, because they are unable to make their votes effective at the ballot-box, the party or State by which they are thus wronged will not be allowed to take advantage of, and enjoy the fruits thereof. They will at least have the satisfaction of knowing that if they cannot vote themselves, others cannot vote for them, and thus appropriate to themselves the increased representation in Congress and in the electoral college to which the State is entitled, based upon their representative strength.

" The strongest point in favor of this proposed change, as I have endeavored to show, grows out of the apparent inequality in representation in the National Convention due to the denial of access to the ballot-box to Republicans through an evasion of the Fifteenth Amendment. I cannot believe, Mr. Chairman, that this convention can be induced to favorably consider any proposition, the effect of which will be to sanction and approve the questionable methods by which the colored Republicans in several Southern States have been disfranchised. I cannot believe that this convention can be induced to favorably consider any proposition, the effect of which will be the sending of a message of sympathy and encouragement to the Democrats of North Carolina, who are now engaged in an effort to disfranchise the colored Republicans of that State.

" The colored Americans ask no special favors as a class,— and no special protection as a race. All they ask and insist upon is equal civil and political rights, and a voice in the government under which they live, and to which they owe allegiance, and for the support of which they are taxed. They feel that they are entitled to such consideration and treatment, not as a matter of favor but as a matter of right.   They came to the rescue of their country when its flag was trailing in the dust of treason and rebellion, and freely watered the tree of liberty with the precious and patriotic blood that flowed from their loyal veins.

"There sits upon the floor of this convention to-day a distinguished gentleman whose name is upon the lips of every patriotic American citizen.   The gentleman to whom I refer, is the member from the great and important State of New York, Theodore Roosevelt, who, as the brave leader of the American troops, led the charge upon San Juan Hill.   In following the lead of that gallant officer on that momentous occasion, the colored American again vindicated his right to a voice in the government of his country.   In his devotion to the cause of liberty and justice the colored American has shown that he was not only willing and ready at any and all times to sacrifice his life upon the altar of his own country, but that he is also willing to fight side by side with his white American brother in an effort to plant the tree of liberty upon a foreign soil.   Must it now be said, that, in spite of all this, the colored American finds himself without a home, without a country, without friends, and even without a party?   God forbid!

"Mr. Chairman, the colored American has been taught to believe that when all other parties and

organizations are against him, he can always look
with hope and encouragement to conventions of the
Republican party. Must that hope now be destroyed? Must he now be made to feel and to
realize the unpleasant fact that, as an American
citizen, his ambition, his hopes and his aspirations
are to be buried beneath the sod of disappointment
and despair? Mr. Chairman, the achievements of
the Republican party as the friend and champion
of equal civil and political rights for all classes
of American citizens, constitute one of the most
brilliant chapters in the history of that grand and
magnificent organization. Must that chapter now
be blotted out? Are you now prepared to confess
that in these grand and glorious achievements the
party made a grave mistake?

" It was a most beautiful and imposing scene that
took place yesterday when a number of venerable
men who took part in the organization of the Republican party, occupied seats upon the platform of
this convention. The presence of those men brought
to mind pleasant and agreeable recollections of the
past. Until the Republican party was organized,
the middle classes, the laboring people, the oppressed
and the slave had no channel through which to
reach the bar of public opinion. The Democratic
party was controlled by the slave oligarchy of the
South, whilst the Whig party had not the courage
of its convictions. The Republican party came to

the front with a determination to secure, if possible, freedom for the slave, liberty for the oppressed, and justice and fair play for all classes and races of our population.   That its efforts in these directions have not been wholly in vain are among the most glorious and brilliant achievements that will constitute a most important part of the history of our country; for it had been the unmistakable determination of that party to make this beautiful country of ours in truth and in fact the land of the free and the home of the brave.   Surely it is not your purpose now to reverse and undo any part of the grand and noble work that has been so successfully and so well done along these lines.

" And yet that is just what you will have done if you adopt the proposition presented by the distinguished gentleman from Pennsylvania.   While I do not assert and cannot believe that such was or is the purpose and desire of the author of that proposition, yet no one that will give the matter careful consideration can fail to see that the effect of it will be to undo, in part at least, what the Republican party has accomplished since its organization.   As a colored Republican, speaking in behalf of that class of our fellow citizens who honor and revere the Republican party for what it has accomplished in the past, I feel that I have a right to appeal to you not to cloud the magnificent record which this grand organization has made.   So far as the colored man is concerned, you found him a slave; you have made him a free man.   You found him a serf; you have made him a sovereign.   You found him a dependent menial; you have made him a soldier.   I therefore appeal to the members of this Convention, in the name of the history of the Republican party, and in behalf of justice and fairplay, to vote down this unjust, unfair, unwise and unnecessary proposition which has been presented by the distinguished gentleman from Pennsylvania."

CHAPTER XXX

ARGUMENT ON PROPOSED CHANGE OF REPRESENTA-
TION IN CONVENTION

In addition to the reasons already given there are many others that might be urged against the proposed change of representation.

In the first place, the present plan is based upon the sound and stable principle upon which the Government was organized. Representation in Congress is not based upon votes or voters, but upon population. The same is true of the different State Legislatures. All political parties,— or, at any rate, the principal ones,— have adopted the same system in the make-up of their State and National Conventions. The membership of the National Convention being based upon each State's representation in Congress, the State Conventions, with perhaps a few exceptions, are based upon the representation in the State Legislatures from each county, parish, or other civil division. It is the fairest, safest, best, and most equitable plan that can be devised or adopted.

Under this plan or system, no State, section or locality can gain or lose representation in any party convention through the application of extraneous or questionable methods, either by the action of the government or of a political party. The representation in Congress and in the different State Legislatures, which is based upon population, fixes the representation from each State in the different National Conventions and in many of the State Conventions. Any other plan or system,— especially that which is based upon the number of votes cast for the candidates of the party as officially ascertained and declared,— would have a tendency to work serious injustice to certain States and sections. In fact, it would have a tendency to sectionalize the party by which the change is made.

Under the present system, for instance, Pennsylvania and Texas have the same representation in a National Democratic Convention that they have in a National Republican Convention, although one is usually Republican in National elections and the other Democratic. And why should not the representation from those States be the same in both conventions? Why should Texas, because it is believed to be safely Democratic, have more power and influence in a Democratic Convention on that account than the Republican State of Pennsylvania? The answer may be because one is a Democratic and the other a Republican State — because one can be relied upon to give its electoral votes to the candidates of the Democratic party while the other can-

not.   But this is not in harmony with our governmental system.   Representation in Congress being
based upon population, every State, section and locality has its relative weight and influence in the
government in accordance with the number of its
inhabitants.

That this is the correct principle will not be seriously questioned when it is carefully considered.
What is true of Pennsylvania and Texas in a National Democratic Convention is equally true of the
same States in a National Republican Convention,
and for the same reasons.   The argument that
Pennsylvania should have relatively a larger representation in a National Republican Convention than
Texas, because the former is reliably Republican
while the latter is hopelessly Democratic, is just
as fallacious in this case as in the other.   But it is
said that delegates from States that cannot contribute to the success of the ticket should not have a
potential voice in nominating a ticket that other
States must be depended upon to elect.   Then why
not exclude them altogether, and also those from
the territories and the District of Columbia?

The argument is unsound, and unreasonable; a
State may be reliably Republican at one election and
yet go Democratic at the next.   In 1872 General
Grant, the Republican candidate for President, carried nearly every State in the Union, in the South as
well as in the North.   Four years later Governor

Hayes, the Republican candidate for President, came within one vote of being defeated in the electoral college; and even then his election was made possible only through the decision of the Electoral Commission. In 1880 General Garfield, the Republican candidate for President, carried New York, and was elected; while four years later Mr. Blaine, the candidate of the same party, lost it and was defeated. In 1888 Harrison, the Republican Presidential candidate, carried New York, and was elected; four years later he not only lost New York, but also such important States as Indiana and Illinois, and came within a few votes of losing Ohio. This was due to a slump in the Republican vote throughout the country, which would have made a very radical change in the National Convention of 1896 if the apportionment of delegates to that convention had been based upon the votes cast for Harrison in 1892. While McKinley, the Republican Presidential candidate, was elected by a large majority in 1896, he lost such important Western States as Kansas, Nebraska, Colorado, Montana, Washington and Nevada. While he was reëlected four years later by an increased majority, he again lost some of the same States. While Roosevelt, the Republican Presidential candidate in 1904, carried every State that McKinley carried in 1900, and several others besides, Mr. Bryan, the Democratic candidate in 1908, though defeated by a large majority, regained some of the Western States that Roosevelt carried in 1904,— notably his own State of Nebraska.

There was a time when such States as Delaware, Maryland, West Virginia, Kentucky, Missouri, and Tennessee were as safely Democratic as Texas and Georgia. Will anyone assert that such is true of them now? There also was a time when such States as Nebraska, Colorado and Nevada were as reliably Republican as Pennsylvania and Vermont. Is that true of them now? In addition to these, taking into consideration important elections that have been held since 1880, the Republicans cannot absolutely rely upon the support of such States as Massachusetts, Maine, Connecticut, New York, New Jersey, Indiana, Illinois, Kansas, and even Ohio. Even the strong Republican State of Pennsylvania has occasionally gone Democratic in what is called an "off year." Other Republican States,— or States that usually go Republican,— have gone Democratic when it was not an off year,— Illinois, for instance, in 1892. All of this goes to prove how unreliable, unsafe, unsatisfactory, unjust and unfair would be the change in the basis of representation as thus proposed.

Another argument in support of the proposed change is that delegates from Democratic States are, as a rule, controlled by the administration then in power, if Republican, and that such delegates can be depended upon to support the administration candidate whoever he may be, regardless of merit, strength or availability. This argument, of course, is based upon the assumption that what is true of Democratic States in this respect is not true of Republican States. The slightest investigation will easily establish the fallacy of this assumption. The truth is that the federal office-holders — especially those holding appointive offices,— can, with a few exceptions, always be depended upon to support the Administration candidate, whoever he may be. The only difference between the North and the South in this respect is that in some of the Southern States, where but one party is allowed to exist,— the Democratic party,— the Republican office-holders can more easily manipulate and control the conventions of their party in such States. But that the office-holders of all sections constitute an important factor in the election of delegates to the National Conventions will not be denied by those who are familiar with the facts, and are honest enough to admit them.

For purposes of illustration we will take the National Republican Convention of 1908, which nominated Judge Taft. It was known that Judge Taft was the man whose candidacy was supported by the Administration. The proceedings of the Convention revealed the fact that outside of five States that had what were called " favorite son " candidates of their own, there were perhaps not more than fifty votes in the whole Convention that were opposed to the administration candidate, although it is more than probable that Judge Taft would not have been nominated but for the fact that he was the choice of the administration.

I am sure no fair-minded person will assert that, in thus voting, the delegates from the Democratic States were influenced by the administration, while those from Republican States were not. It is not my purpose to assert or even intimate that any questionable methods were used to influence the election, or control the votes of the delegates in the interest of any one candidate. Nothing of that sort was necessary, since human nature is the same the world over.

That the office-holders should be loyal to the administration to which they belong is perfectly natural. That those who wish to become office-holders should be anxious to be on the winning side is also natural, and that, too, without regard to the locality or section in which they live. It is a fact, therefore, that up to 1908 no candidate has ever been nominated by a Republican National Convention who did not finally receive a sufficient number of votes from all sections of the country to make his nomination practically the choice of the party without regard to sectional lines.

If, then, it be a fact that in 1908, for instance,

delegates to the National Republican Convention were elected and controlled through administration influences in the interest of any one candidate, such influences were no less potential in Republican than in Democratic States. Outside of the administration candidate there were at that Convention five very important States that presented candidates of their own. They were New York, Indiana, Illinois, Pennsylvania, and Wisconsin. That the delegation from each of said States were practically solid in the support of its " favorite son " was due largely to the wise decision of the managers of the administration candidate to concede to each of said " favorite sons " the delegation from his own State without a contest. But for this decision, which was wisely made in the interest of party harmony, no one of those " favorite sons " would have had the solid delegation from his own State. As it was, a large majority of the delegates from the five States named was not unfriendly to the Administration candidate. These delegates voted for their " favorite sons " simply because they knew that in doing so they were not antagonizing the administration. There never was a time, therefore, when they could have been united upon any one candidate in opposition to the one that had at his back the powerful support of the Administration. Our government has reached that point in its growth, where it is not only possible, but compara-

tively easy, for an administration to secure the
nomination of the one by whom it desires to be
succeeded,— especially under the present system of
electing delegates. It was in anticipation of this,
and to prevent any one man from perpetuating himself in power, that Washington established the precedent against a third successive term.

If the advocates of this proposed change are to
be believed, and if they wish to be consistent, they
should include the National Committee. The composition of that body is somewhat similar to that
of the United States Senate. In the Senate Nevada
and Delaware have the same representation as New
York and Pennsylvania. In the National Committee each State, territory, and the District of Columbia has one vote. If any change in the interest of
reform is necessary, the National Republican Committee is the organization where it should first be
made; for it often happens that that committee can
not only shape the policy of the party but control the
nomination as well,— especially when the result between opposing candidates is close and doubtful.
In such a contest the candidate that has the support
of a majority of the National Committee has a decided advantage over his rivals for the nomination.
If the result should be close that advantage will be
more than likely to secure him the nomination.

The National Committee prepares the roll of the
delegates to the Convention, and, in doing so, it de-

cides primarily every contested seat. If the contests thus decided should give any one candidate a majority, that majority will be sure to retain the advantage thus secured. It will thus be seen that if any change is necessary this is the place where it should first be made. It occurs to me that instead of changing the basis of representation the most effective remedy for the evils now complained of is to have the delegates to National Conventions elected at popular primaries, instead of by State and district conventions.

CHAPTER XXXI

COMPARISON OF BRYAN AND CLEVELAND

It was upon the territory which now comprises the States of Kansas and Nebraska that the preliminary battles in the interest of freedom were successfully fought. This is especially true of that part of the territory which now comprises the State of Kansas. But not only for that reason has that State occupied a prominent place before the public; other events of national importance have had their birth there. It was Kansas that furnished one of the Republican United State Senators who voted against the conviction, of Andrew Johnson,— who had been impeached by the House of Representatives for high crimes and misdemeanors in office,— and thus secured the President's acquittal. That State also furnished one of the most remarkable men that ever occupied a seat in the United States Senate, John J. Ingalls.

I distinctly remember him as an able and brilliant young Senator when,— in 1875, under the leadership of Senator George F. Edmunds, of Vermont,— he took a prominent part in the successful fight that was made in that body to secure the passage of the

Sumner Civil Rights Bill. It was this fight that demonstrated his fitness for the position he subsequently occupied as one of the distinguished leaders on the Republican side of the Senate. He was a natural born orator, having a wonderful command of the English language; and, while he was somewhat superficial and not always logical, he never failed to be interesting, though he was seldom instructive. For severe satire and irony he had few equals and no superiors. It was on this account that no Senator was anxious to get into a controversy with him. But for two unfortunate events in the career of John J. Ingalls he would have filled a much more important position in the history of his country than it is now possible for the impartial historian to give him.

Kansas, unfortunately, proved to be a fertile field for the growth and development of that ephemeral organization known as the Populist party,— a party that had secured a majority in the Legislature that was to elect the successor to Mr. Ingalls. The Senator evidently had great confidence in his own oratorical ability. He appeared to have conceived the idea that it was possible for him to make a speech on the floor of the Senate that would insure his reëlection even by a Populist Legislature. In this,— as he soon found out, to his bitter disappointment,— he was mistaken. He no doubt came to the same conclusion that many of his friends and admirers had already come to, that in bidding for the support of the Populists of his State he had made the mistake of his life. The impression he made upon the public mind was that he was devoid of principle, and that he was willing to sacrifice his own party upon the altar of his ambition.

But it was neither known nor suspected that he contemplated making a bid for the support of the Populist members of the Legislature until he delivered his speech. When, therefore, it was announced that Senator Ingalls would address the Senate on a certain day, he was greeted, as on previous occasions, with a large audience. But this was the first time that his hearers had been sadly disappointed. This was due more to what was said than how it was said. Then it was plain to those who heard him that his heart was not in what he was saying; hence the speech was devoid of that fiery eloquence which on previous occasions had charmed and electrified his hearers. But, after that speech, when one of his auditors would ask another what he thought of it, the reply invariably was a groan of disappointment. When the immense crowd dispersed at the conclusion of the speech instead of smiling faces and pleasing countenances as on previous occasions, one could not help noticing marked evidences of disappointment in every face. The impression that had been made was, that it was an appeal to the Populist members of the Legislature of

his State to return him to the Senate, in exchange
for which he was willing to turn his back upon the
party which he was then serving. It was almost
equivalent to an open declaration of his willingness
to identify himself with the Populists, and champion
their cause if they would reëlect him to the seat
he then occupied. From the effects of that fatal
blunder the Senator never recovered.

Another thing that lessened the distinguished
orator and Senator in the estimation of the public
was his radically changed attitude upon questions
affecting the political, social and industrial status
of the colored Americans. From a brilliant and
eloquent champion and defender of their civil and
political rights he became one of their most severe
critics. From his latest utterances upon that subject it was clear to those who heard what he said
that the colored Americans merited nothing that
had been said and done in their behalf, but nearly
everything that had been said and done against
them. Why there had been such a radical change
in his attitude upon that subject, has been an inexplicable mystery. The only explanation that I
have heard from the lips of some of his former
friends and admirers was that it was in the nature
of an experiment,— the expectation being that it
would give him a sensational fame throughout the
country, which could be utilized to his financial advantage upon his retirement to private life. This

explanation would have been rejected without serious consideration, but for the fact that some others have pursued the same course for the same reason, and their hopes have been, in a large measure, realized. In his bid for the support of the Populist members of the Legislature of his State the Senator had established the fact that he did not have very strong convictions upon any subject, and that those he had could be easily changed to suit the times and the occasion.

Nebraska, though not very strong politically, is one of the most important States in the West. It has sent a number of men to the front who have made an impression upon the public mind. For many years no State in the Union was more reliably Republican than Nebraska. A large majority of its voters, I am sure, are not now in harmony with the Democratic party,— nor have they ever been so,— but it is true, at the same time, that thousands of those who for many years acted with the Republican party, and voted for its candidates, have become alienated, thus making Republican success at any election in the State close and doubtful, and that, too, regardless of the merits of opposing candidates or the platform declarations of opposing parties.

For this remarkable change there must be a good and sufficient reason. The State in its early history was sparsely populated, and stood very much

in need of railroads for the development of its re-
sources. In those days, railroads were very popular, and the people were in a mood to offer liberal
inducements to those who would raise the means
to furnish them with the necessary transportation
facilities.

For the same reason the Federal Government
made valuable concessions in the interest of railroad construction in the Western States. Since the
railroads, thus aided, were in a large measure the
creatures of the State and Nation they thereby acquired an interest in the administration of the National and State Governments,— especially those of
the State,— that they otherwise would not have had.

The construction of the roads went on at such
a rapid rate that they soon acquired such a power
and influence in the administration of the State
Government that the people looked upon it as being dangerous to their liberties. In fact it was
claimed,— a claim, no doubt, largely supported by
the facts,— that the State Government was actually
dominated by railroad influence. No one, it was
said, could be elected or appointed to an important
office who was not acceptable to the railroad interests. This state of affairs produced a revulsion
among the common people; thousands of whom
decided that they would vote against the Republican party, which was then,— as it had been for
many years,— in control of the State Government

because of its having allowed such a state of affairs to be brought about.

Edward Rosewater, editor and proprietor of the Omaha *Bee,* the most influential Republican paper in the State, took sides against the railroad interests. The result was that Nebraska, for the first time, elected a Democratic governor.

But many of the Republicans who acted with the Democrats on that occasion could not see their way clear to remain in that party, though some of them were not willing to return to the ranks of the Republicans. So they decided to cast their lot with the Populist party, which in the meantime had made its appearance upon the field of political activity. While the Democratic party remained the minority party in the State, it was seldom that the Republicans could poll more votes than the Democrats and Populists combined, and since, under the then leadership of the Democratic party in the State, that party and the Populist stood practically for the same things, it was not difficult to bring about fusion of the two parties against the Republicans. This gave the Fusionists control of the State Government for a number of years.

In the meantime a brilliant, eloquent and talented young man had come upon the stage of political activity. This man was William J. Bryan. His first entry into public life was his election to Congress as a Democrat from a Republican district. While a member of the House he made a speech on the tariff question which gave him national fame. As a speaker William Jennings Bryan has always been plausible and captivating. He can clothe his thoughts in such beautiful and eloquent language that he seldom fails to make a favorable impression upon those who hear him. It was this wonderful faculty that secured him his first nomination for the Presidency. His name was hardly thought of in connection with the nomination by that convention. In fact his right to a seat as a member of the convention was disputed and contested. But, after he had delivered his cross of gold and crown of thorns speech before that body, he carried the Convention by storm. His nomination was then a foregone conclusion.

It was under the leadership and chiefly through the influence of Mr. Bryan that the fusion between the Democrats and the Populists of his State was brought about. But for his advocacy of Free Silver and his affiliation with the Populists, he might have reached the goal of his ambition. The result of the election showed that while he commanded and received the support of not less than eighty per cent of his own party, the remaining twenty per cent proved to be strong enough to insure his defeat. In fact the business interests of the country were almost solid against him; and it is safe to say that no man can ever hope to become President

of the United States who cannot at least divide
the substantial and solid business interests. The
business men were apprehensive that the election
of Mr. Bryan would bring about financial and commercial disaster, hence they, almost regardless of
previous party affiliations, practically united in an
effort to defeat him.

The State of Nebraska, therefore, will always occupy a prominent place in the history of the country, because,— though young, small, and politically
weak,— it has produced the most remarkable man
of whom the Democratic party can boast. It has
also produced a number of very able men on the Republican side, such men, for instance, as C. F. Manderson, and John M. Thurston,— who both served
the State in the United States Senate, and made
brilliant records. But Mr. Bryan had an advantage over these two when he stood before a popular
audience in Nebraska, because they had been identified with the railroad interests, while he had not.

That Mr. Bryan is a strong man and has a wonderful hold upon his party is shown by the fact that
he has been three times the party candidate for the
Presidency. While it may be true that he can
never be elected to the Presidency, it is no doubt
equally true that while he lives no other Democrat
can become President who is not acceptable to him
and to his friends.

In one respect at least, Mr. Cleveland and Mr.

Bryan were very much alike. As already stated, Mr. Bryan is a Democrat. The same was true of Mr. Cleveland; and yet they were as radically different as it is possible for two men to be. They were not only different in temperament and disposition, but also in their views and convictions upon public questions,— at least, so far as the public is informed,—with the possible exception of the tariff. There was another question that came to the front after the Spanish American war,— the question of "Imperialism,"— upon which they may have been in accord; but this is not positively known to be a fact. Indeed, the tariff is such a complicated subject that they may not have been in perfect accord even on that. Mr. Cleveland was elected President in 1892 upon a platform pledged to a tariff for revenue only. The Democrats had a majority in both Houses of Congress; but when that majority passed a tariff bill, it fell so far short of Mr. Cleveland's idea of a tariff for revenue only that he not only denounced it in strong language, but refused to sign it. Whether or not Mr. Bryan was with the President or with the Democratic majority in Congress in that fight is not known; but, judging from his previous public utterances upon the subject, it is to be presumed that he was in accord with the President.

It is claimed by the friends and admirers of both Mr. Cleveland and Mr. Bryan that each could be truly called a Jeffersonian Democrat; which means a strong advocate and defender of what is called States Rights, a doctrine on which is based one of the principal differences between the Republican and Democratic parties. Yet President Cleveland did not hesitate to use the military force of the government to suppress domestic violence within the boundaries of a State, and that too against the protest of the Governor of the State, for the alleged reason that such action was necessary to prevent the interruption of the carrying of the United States mail. Mr. Bryan's views upon the same subject appear to be sufficiently elastic to justify the National Government, in his opinion, in becoming the owner and operator of the principal railroads of the country. His views along those lines are so far in advance of those of his party that he was obliged, for reasons of political expediency and party exigency, to hold them in abeyance during the Presidential campaign of 1908. Jeffersonian democracy, therefore, seems now to be nothing more than a meaningless form of expression.

CHAPTER XXXII

THE SOLID SOUTH, PAST AND PRESENT.   FUTURE OF THE REPUBLICAN PARTY

To turn again to the South. This section has been a fertile field for political experimental purposes by successive Republican administrations, ever since the second administration of President Grant. The Solid South, so-called, has been a serious menace to the peace and prosperity of the country. How to bring about such a condition of affairs as would do away with the supposed necessity for its continuance has been the problem, the solution of which has been the cause of political experiments. President Hayes was the first to try the experiment of appointing Democrats to many of the most important offices, hoping that the solution would thus be found. But he was not given credit for honest motives in doing so, for the reason that the public was impressed with the belief that such action on his part was one of the conditions upon which he was allowed to be peaceably inaugurated. At any rate the experiment was a complete failure, hence, so far as the more important offices were concerned, that policy was not continued by Republican administrations that came into power subsequent to the Hayes administration, and prior to that of Taft's.

I do not mean to say that no Democrats were appointed to important offices at the South by the administrations referred to, but such appointments were not made with the belief or expectation that they would contribute to a solution of the problem that was involved in what was known as the Solid South. Political and social conditions in that section of the country are such that the appointment to some of the federal offices of men who are not identified with the Republican party is inevitable. The impression that the writer desires to make upon the mind of the reader is that, between the administration of Hayes and that of Taft no Republican administrations made such appointments with the expectation that they would contribute to a breaking up of the solid south. President Roosevelt tried the experiment of offering encouragement and inducements in that direction to what was known as the Gold-standard Democrats, but even that was barren of satisfactory results. President Taft seems to be the only Republican President since Mr. Hayes who has allowed himself to labor under the delusion that the desired result could be accomplished through the use and distribution of Federal patronage. The chief mistake on the part of those who thus believe, and who act in accordance with that belief, grows out of a serious lack of information about the actual situation. In the first place their action is based upon the assumption that the Solid South,— or what remains of it,— is an outgrowth of an honest expression of the wishes of the people of that section, whereas, in point of fact, the masses had very little to do with bringing about present conditions and know less about them. Those conditions are not due primarily to the fact that colored men are intimidated by white men, but that white men are intimidated by the Democratic party. They are not due primarily to the fact that colored men are disfranchised, but that white men are prevented from giving effective expression to their honest political opinions and convictions.

The disfranchisement of the colored men is one of the results growing out of those conditions, which would not and could not exist if there were absolute freedom of thought and action in political matters among the white people. The only part that the so-called Race Question plays in this business is that it is used as a pretext to justify the coercive and proscriptive methods thus used. The fact that the colored man is disfranchised and has no voice in the creation and administration of the government under which he lives and by which he is taxed does not change the situation in this respect. His presence,— whether he can vote or not, — furnishes the occasion for the continuance of such methods, and, as long as intelligent persons, especially at the North and particularly in the Republican party, can be thus fooled and deceived they will not be discontinued.

The announcement of President Taft's Southern policy, therefore, was received by the present leaders of the Democratic party at the South with satisfaction and delight, not on account of the official recognition that members of their party were to receive, for that was of secondary importance, but on account of the fact that they could clearly see that their contention about the so-called race question was thus given a national sanction, which would have the effect of making that question serve them for several more Presidential campaigns. It was giving a new market value to this " watered stock," from which they would derive political dividends for a much longer period than they otherwise would. They could thus see to their unbounded glee that if a man of President Taft's intelligence and experience could thus be deceived as to conditions at the South, they would not have very much difficulty in deceiving others who were not believed to be so well informed.

To solve this problem, therefore, the disposition of the federal patronage will cut a very small figure. The patronage question is not half so important, in a political or party sense, as many have been led to believe. It really makes very little difference by whom the few offices are held, whether they be all Democrats, all Republicans, some white, some colored, provided they be honest, capable, and efficient. For political, personal or party reasons some feeling may be created, and some prejudice may be aroused on account of the appointment of a certain person to an office; but if no attention should be paid to it, and the fact should be developed that the duties of the same are being discharged in a creditable and satisfactory manner the public will soon forget all about it. The fact remains, however, that the disposition of the federal patronage will not produce the slightest change in the political situation in such localities. If a national Republican administration should refuse to appoint a colored man, for instance, to any office in any one of the Southern States for the alleged reason that it might be objectionable to the white people of the community,— and therefore might have a tendency to prevent white men from coming into the Republican party, — at the very next election in that community the fact would be demonstrated that the Republican party had not gained and that the Democratic party had not lost a single vote as a result thereof. The reason for this result would be in the first place that the excuse given was insincere and untrue, and in the second place, because the incumbent of the office, whoever he might be, would produce no effect whatsoever in the local situation in consequence of his appointment to the office and his acceptance of it. If there should be any change at all in the situation it would doubtless be to the detriment of the Republican party; for there would, no doubt, be some who would be disposed to resent what would seem to them to be political or party ingratitude.

So far as the colored Republicans are concerned they have been in the past, and must be in the future, nothing more than party allies. They have never dominated a State, nor have they controlled the Republican organization of any State to the exclusion of the white men thereof. They have simply been the allies of white men who could be induced to come forward and assume the leadership. This is all they have been in the past; it is all they desire to be in the future. They are perfectly willing to follow where others lead provided those others lead wisely and in the right direction. All they ask, desire and insist upon is to be recognized as political allies upon terms of equality and to have a voice in the councils of the party of their choice and in the creation and administration of the government under which they live, and by which they are taxed, and also a fair and reasonable recognition as a result of party success, based, all things else being equal, upon merit, fitness, ability and capacity. Even in States where it is possible for them to wield a sufficient influence to be potential in party conventions, and to help shape the policy and select the candidates of that party, they never fail to support the strongest and best men among the white members of the organization. If it be true that they were sometimes the victims of misplaced confidence, it cannot, and will not, be denied that the same is equally true of white men of far more experience in such matters.

If there is ever to be again, as there once was, a strong and substantial Republican party at the South, or a party by any other name that will openly oppose the ruling oligarchy of that section,— as I have every reason to believe will eventually take place,— it will not be through the disposition of federal patronage, but in consequence of the acceptance by the people of that section of the principles and policies for which the National Organization stands. For the accomplishment of this purpose and for the attainment of this end time is the most important factor. Questionable methods that have been used to hold in abeyance the advancing civilization of the age will eventually be overcome and effectually destroyed. The wheels of progress, of intelligence, and of right cannot and will not move backwards, but will go forward in spite of all that can be said and done. In the mean time the exercise of patience, forbearance, and good judgment are all that will be required.

Another fact which seems to be overlooked by many is that the so-called Solid South of to-day is not the menace to the country that it was between 1875 and 1888.   During that period the Solid South included the States of Delaware, Maryland, West Virginia, Kentucky, and Missouri.   Those States at that time were as reliably Democratic as Texas and Georgia.   Such does not seem to be true of them now, and yet I venture the assertion that the disposition of the federal patronage in them had very little, if anything, to do with bringing about the change.   What has been done and is being done in those States can be done in others that are located south of them.   As strong as the Republican party is there is one thing it cannot afford to do, and that is to encourage or tolerate the drawing of the race or color line in any efforts that may be made to break up and dissolve what now remains of the Solid South.   One of the cardinal principles and doctrines of the Republican party,— the principle that has, more than any other, secured for it the loyal and consistent support of those who represent the moral sentiment of the country,— is its bold and aggressive advocacy and defense of liberty, justice, and equal civil and political rights for all classes of American citizens.   From that grand and noble position it cannot afford to descend in an effort to find new and doubtful allies.   If it should in an evil moment allow itself to make such a grave blunder, such a criminal mistake, it will thereby forfeit the confidence and support of the major part of those upon whom in the past it has relied,— and never in vain,— for its continuance in power. There is nothing in the situation that would justify the experiment, even if it were thought that a little temporary and local advantage would be secured thereby.

The Fifteenth Amendment to the National Constitution was not intended to confer suffrage upon any particular race or class of persons, but merely to place a limit upon the National Government and that of the several States in prescribing the qualifications of electors.   Whatever power the national or any state government may have had in prescribing the qualification of electors prior to the ratification of the Fifteenth Amendment it still has, save that it cannot legally and constitutionally make race or color a ground of disqualificaion.   In other words, whatever qualifications may be prescribed and fixed as a condition precedent to voting, must be applicable to white and colored alike.   A few States, under the false plea of political necessity, have resorted to certain schemes of doubtful constitutionality, for the sole purpose of evading this plain provision of the National Constitution.   They may stand for a while, but, even if they could stand indefinitely, that fact would furnish no excuse for the party,— a party that has stood so long, and fought so hard for liberty, justice, equal rights, and fair play,— to enter into a political alliance with any other party or faction which would involve a compromise or an abandonment of those grand and noble principles. The Republican party is still in the prime and glory of its usefulness. It is still strong in the confidence and affections of the masses of the people, at least such was the case in 1908, because it had not up to that time allowed itself to compromise or abandon,— so far as its platform utterances were concerned,— the fundamental principles which called it into existence and which caused it to be placed in control of the National Government, and which have caused its continuance in power for so many years. Whether or not the unwise and unfortunate southern policy inaugurated by the Taft Administration will result in disaster to the party is not and cannot be known at this writing. We can only hope.

THE END